GREAT LAKES
PIRATE

GREAT LAKES
PIRATE

THE ADVENTURES
OF ROARING DAN SEAVEY

GAVIN SCHMITT

THE
History
PRESS

Published by The History Press
Charleston, SC
www.historypress.com

Copyright © 2021 by Gavin Schmitt
All rights reserved

Front cover: Chicago Historical Museum.
Back cover, top: Library of Congress; *bottom*: Library of Congress.

First published 2021

Manufactured in the United States

ISBN 9781467146173

Library of Congress Control Number: 2020951675

Notice: The information in this book is true and complete to the best of our knowledge. It is offered without guarantee on the part of the author or The History Press. The author and The History Press disclaim all liability in connection with the use of this book.

For Liz
Your smile is worth more than all of the world's buried treasure.

CONTENTS

INTRODUCTION

Daniel Seavey, sometimes called "Roaring Dan," is a legendary, almost mythical figure in the history of Lake Michigan and the Great Lakes. Author Thomas Edward Jacques speaks of the "legend" in a blunt manner. He says we can know only "two undeniable facts" about Seavey: that he was born and that he died. That is not far from the mark. But even here the facts get murky, as we'll soon discover. Seavey was well known in his day in northeast Wisconsin and the Upper Peninsula of Michigan, for both good and bad reasons, and more often than not for things that probably never happened. He was a folk hero to some, a demon to others. But are the stories we know "undeniable facts?"

Local historian John Mitchell, at a lecture he gave in 1961, puts the blend of fact and fiction another way. He says, "If you start cleaning up Dan Seavey you have to be careful, because if you go too far, you won't have much left." In many ways, Seavey *is* the collection of rumors and innuendos, even if they may not have that kernel of truth. Mitchell concludes, "We do know, however, that he was a rough, tough barroom brawler, expert with fists and boots, a fearless sailor. A conscienceless ruffian on one hand, a kind generous rough-and-ready type on the other."

Today, where he is still known, he is remembered as a pirate with all the stereotypes that such a label entails. Specifically, he is credited with being "the only man to be arrested for piracy on Lake Michigan"—some say the only man to be "convicted" of such a charge. On the extreme end, he has been called the only pirate on the lake, period. Indeed, his legendary status has allowed him the greatest posthumous honor: a liquor is named for him, thanks to Great Lakes Distillery of Milwaukee. Appropriately enough for a pirate, you can get a bottle of Roaring Dan's Rum.

The truth is both more mundane and more exciting. To find that truth, one has to completely deconstruct the legend and rebuild the man from scratch. The juiciest stories about Seavey simply have no documentation, and while they make excellent folklore, they are terrible history. The newspapers of the day never shied away from bloody rumors, and with each new telling, the body count grows. The tall tales told about Seavey may very well be true, but the historian cannot rely on stories passed from one generation to the next. Primary sources are key. Today, it is quite possible no one still alive has ever met the man, and we are left with only a scant paper trail.

The pirate tales—despite being Seaver's claim to fame—are greatly exaggerated. He was not convicted of piracy, and whether he was even arrested under such a charge is open to debate. We will discuss it more thoroughly later. Seavey being the only pirate on Lake Michigan is almost certainly false, depending on how one defines the term *pirate*. If one has to be arrested for "piracy" to be a pirate, he may be unique. But pirate-like figures were common around Beaver Island in the days of the Mormon settlement under James Jesse Strang, a story worth its own book or three. During Prohibition, smuggling alcohol across the lake was not unheard of. Is a smuggler all that different from a pirate?

Years later, a "weather beaten" sailor—not otherwise identified—regaled the *Oswego Palladium* with his Great Lakes tales. "The lakes have had pirates in their day," he recalled, referring to the Mormons of Beaver Island. "Several vessels disappeared in that vicinity in mid-summer, and neither they nor their crews were ever heard from. It was said that the Mormons boarded becalmed vessels, murdered the crews, discharged the cargoes on the island and burned or scuttled the craft."

Other parts of the Seavey story have been glossed over, overshadowed by the piracy angle. These other tales are just as fascinating or even more so. He was a man who befriended the Pabst brewing family, took part in the Alaskan gold rush, survived an exploding sawmill and navigated through numerous dangerous storms in a time before now-ubiquitous devices such as two-way radios and electric lights (not to mention cellphones) were commonplace. Seavey was in many ways more than a man, but rather the very archetype of the American pioneer.

In this book, we will explore themes of human adventure and exploration while also shedding light on overlooked and forgotten American history. With Captain Seavey as our guide, we may get off course to inspect tangents of the story, but we'll make it to our destination...eventually.

1

THE BEGATS

In many ways, the story of the Seavey family is the story of America and its rugged individualism, as Herbert Hoover would later observe—from the country's colonial settlement, through westward expansion, to the wilds of the Yukon and beyond. While the story of Dan Seavey specifically is one worth telling, his tale becomes even more interesting when put in the broad historical context of many generations.

In the beginning, Captain John Mason of Norfolk, England, sent fifty-eight men and twenty-two women to the Piscataqua River in 1631, in an area that would become the border between New Hampshire and Maine. Mason had once been arrested for piracy in the North Sea but was now ironically tasked with preventing piracy off the shores of Newfoundland. The voyage was a mere decade after the celebrated *Mayflower* landing. The short, twelve-mile Piscataqua River would be a focal point in early British colonization. Explorer Martin Pring had been to the river as early as 1603, and the very first sawmill in the British colonies was built there in 1623. Salmon, sturgeon, oysters, clams, scallops, lobsters, mussels, eels, seals and many other species of marine life were common in the river in those days.

Captain Mason's crew was led by William Berry, who today is credited as the first (White) settler of Rye, Rockingham County, in what would become New Hampshire. Berry gets the credit, but any of those on the same journey, including one William Seavey of Stokeinteignhead, in Devon, England, could equally make the same claim. The Seavey family has been recorded in Stokeinteignhead at least as far back as the 1460s. Despite the longevity of the Seavey clan in England, virtually all members of the family in America can trace their roots to William or his brother Thomas.

Although Captain Mason had previously been governor of Newfoundland and made the first known map of that territory, Mason did not join Berry's crew and never set foot in New England, and yet he was appointed first vice-admiral of the region in 1635. Mason died that same year while preparing for his first voyage to the new colony.

The history of Rye is a complex and convoluted one. Prior to its incorporation almost one hundred years later, Rye was first called Sandy Beach, and its lands were once parts of the communities of today's New Castle, Portsmouth, Greenland and Hampton. In 1726, the town of New Castle set off a new community for Sandy Beach called Rye, named for Rye in Sussex, England. Simply put, the borders and names of these cities changed and shifted over time. A person could live at Sandy Beach, New Castle and Rye at different points in their life without ever leaving their house. For the sake of simplicity, the area will be referred to as Rye and ignore other historical names.

The pioneer William Seavey was granted fifty acres of land in 1652 in Rye on the south side of Mill Creek. Three hundred years later, the property was still in the hands of the Seavey clan. On the death of William Berry in 1669, Seavey purchased more land from the estate of his former captain. This tract connected his property with that of his nephew, one Thomas Seavey, who arrived in Rye sometime after William's voyage. Others say Thomas already arrived in 1631—the same year as William—though he would have been only a child and is not known to have arrived with his uncle. Unfortunately for our purposes, such things as "ship manifests" and "immigration records" are hard to come by in the colonial era.

Thomas Seavey, the nephew, was born around 1627 in Stokeinteignhead, the same village as his uncle; one can assume the English town was a very small community in those days, as the population in 2001 amounted to only 707 inhabitants. His principal residence in America was near Odiorde's Point in Rye. Thomas received property grants in 1652 and, later, purchased more property at Odiorde's Point. Thomas died on February 6, 1707, in Rockingham County, New Hampshire.

Samuel Seavey, the son of Thomas, was born in 1672 in Rye. He was a farmer in Rye, and very little is known about him. Early in his life (1679), King Charles II separated New Hampshire from Massachusetts, issuing a charter for the royal "Province of New Hampshire," with Welsh mill owner John Cutt as president (governor). Cutt died after an illness struck him the same

The Amos Seavey home in Rye, New Hampshire, dating to 1730. *Library of Congress.*

day a comet passed over, leading local politicians to declare this coincidence a sign of "divine displeasure." New Hampshire was next absorbed into the ill-fated Dominion of New England in 1686, which soon collapsed in 1689. How much this political shifting affected the average colonist is open to speculation. Perhaps as a farmer, Samuel Seavey tended his land and paid no attention to the shifting borders. Samuel died about December 1737.

Samuel Seavey II was born in 1690, also in Rye. On October 25, 1711, he married Abigail Foss, the daughter of John Foss and Mary Thadburn. From the time of the couple's marriage, this Seavey generation relocated from Rye to nearby Greenland in Rockingham County. During Samuel's life, laws cementing the institution of slavery were passed in New Hampshire. One law in 1714 declared, "Whereas great disorders, insolencies and burglaries are oft times raised and committed in the night time by Indian, Negro, and Molatto Servants and Slaves to the Disquiet and hurt of her Majesty, No Indian, Negro, or Molatto is to be from Home after 9 o'clock." Though we might generally think of slavery as being firmly rooted in the South on plantations, it is worth noting that slavery was legal in New Hampshire up through 1857. There is no evidence that the Seavey family owned slaves, and no evidence hints at how they felt about the issue one way or the other. Samuel died before September 3, 1761. This is the date his will was "proved," suggesting the death was not long before.

Jonathan Seavey, son of Samuel II, was born on February 2, 1731, in Rye. Jonathan's wife is sometimes given as a member of the extensive Stevens family, or more often as Comfort Cate. The latter has some likelihood, because Jonathan had a daughter also named Comfort. Records suggest that Jonathan and Comfort were married in 1755 at Greenland. This generation moved slightly again from Rockingham County to Rochester in Strafford County. Jonathan allegedly died in Conway, Carroll County, approximately eighty miles due north of Greenland, though no record of this death could be found.

Jonathan Seavey II was born on August 16, 1758, in Greenland. He achieved immortality when he served in the Revolutionary War under Captain Richard Benjamin Shortridge, as part of Colonel Enoch Poor's regiment, from 1775 to 1778.

On May 22, 1775, the New Hampshire Provincial Congress voted to raise a volunteer force to join the Patriot army at Boston. Shortridge raised the first company in Portsmouth for the War of the Revolution, with orders dated June 14, 1775. He was commissioned on June 18, 1775, as Captain of the Tenth Company of the Second New Hampshire Regiment, Continental Line, commanded by Colonel Enoch Poor. Shortridge was in the siege of Boston, stationed on Winter Hill, under the command of Brigadier General John Sullivan, who arrived from Philadelphia on June 27.

General George Washington arrived in Boston on July 2, set up his headquarters at Harvard College and took command of the newly formed Continental army the following day. By this time, forces and supplies were arriving, including companies of riflemen from as far away as Maryland and Virginia. Washington began the work of molding the militias into something more closely resembling an army, appointing senior officers and introducing more organization and disciplinary measures to the encamped militias.

The months wore on with countless skirmishes. The British set fire to taverns, while the Americans killed a British soldier and hanged him on the edge of town as an example. Fishing vessels were used to gather intelligence up and down the coast. As winter approached, the Americans were so short on gunpowder that soldiers were given spears to fight with in the event of a British attack. Many of the American troops remained unpaid, and many of their enlistments would be up at the end of that year.

In December 1775, Captain Shortridge and the majority of his company reenlisted, and bounties were paid by the town of Portsmouth for sixty-one men. New Hampshire's patriotism was strong, and in January 1776, the future state became the first colony to set up an independent government and was the first to establish a constitution. Interestingly, the original constitution had an upper and lower house of congress (as is common), but no governor or chief executive at all. The congress had complete authority to make executive appointments.

Many of the Connecticut companies refused to reenlist or to remain thirty days beyond their time, but Captain Shortridge and his company remained in camp until Boston was evacuated by the British on March 19, 1776. After this success, the regiment went on the expedition to Canada on March 29 under the command of General Sullivan, arriving at Ticonderoga on May 14. Washington had sent Sullivan north to replace the fallen John Thomas as commander in Quebec. He took command of the sick and faltering invasion force, sent some of those forces on an unsuccessful counterattack against the British at Three Rivers and withdrew the survivors to Crown Point. This led to the first of several controversies between Congress and General Sullivan, as the American government sought a scapegoat for the failed invasion of Canada.

Ultimately, Captain Shortridge allegedly died in battle at Gwynn's Island on July 8, 1776. Seavey managed to outlive his superior officer and see the birth of a new nation. Shortridge only "allegedly" died because other sources claim the only casualty on the side of the revolutionaries at Gwynn's Island was one Captain Dohickey Arundel. The commander of two eighteen-pound cannons. Arundel attempted to fire an experimental wood mortar of his own invention, "though the general and all the officers were against his firing it." The mortar exploded on its first shot, killing the unlikely named Arundel instantly. A number of extended Seavey family members also served in the Revolution. Amos Seavey served in a legal capacity, while Joseph Seavey was a sergeant and William Seavey a lieutenant. Given the multiple people using these common names, it is hard to determine the exact relationship they had to Jonathan Seavey.

Jonathan Seavey married Priscilla Philbrick on September 22, 1778. She passed away on May 21, 1823, in Conway; he followed on September 9, 1846, in the same place.

Clement Seavey lived in Waterford, Oxford County, Maine. His birth was in Shelburne, Coos County, on June 15, 1776, a few weeks before independence was declared. He was conceived prior to his parents' marriage;

in fact, he was even born before the marriage. Possibly Jonathan Seavey intended to marry Priscilla Philbrick but was held up a few years by the revolution. Given the available information, it is hard to speculate about how such things as children born out of wedlock—even under unusual circumstances—were perceived at the time.

Clement took out a marriage license with Betsy Boynton in 1797, but it does not appear they followed through. Clement and Hannah Bennett, the daughter of Tilton and Rachel Bennett, were married on March 25, 1798, by Baptist clergyman John T. Crockett in Sanbornton, Belknap County. The ceremony was only six months prior to the birth of their first child, Betsy. There is speculation in the family today that this daughter was named for Betsy Boynton, who may have died between her engagement and marriage with Clement. Furthermore, becoming pregnant prior to marriage may be the reason Clement and Hannah got married in Sanbornton and then moved to Shelburne, eighty to ninety miles away, in order to hide their indiscretion. Clement Seavey very nearly followed the same pattern as his father before him, though this time with less of an excuse.

Clement Seavey shows up in Portsmouth, New Hampshire town records as a taxpayer from 1801 through 1807. He worked for a time as a painter. In 1807, he is listed as owning "two buildings" and "one stock in trade." In 1808, he is listed as "gone" in the tax records. This is consistent with the birth records of their children: Mary Ann (1802), Clarisay (1804) and Susanna (1806) were all born in Portsmouth, but the first son entered the world elsewhere. Clement died on June 17, 1844.

Clement Seavey II was born on December 7, 1807, in Gilead, Oxford County, Maine. Or, rather, in what would soon be Maine—our most northeastern state broke off from Massachusetts in 1820. The reasons for this split are interesting, though largely outside of our scope. Suffice it to say that Maine achieved statehood following Massachusetts' reluctance to secure the border with Canada in the War of 1812. This new state, however, opened the door for Missouri statehood and inched the United States closer to civil war in the process. Clement was married first to Susan Cloutman on December 20, 1829, in Bethel, Oxford County. Susan presumably died young, only about a year into the marriage. Although the exact date of her death is unknown, this is suggested by the fact that Clement next married Janet Rowell of Gorham, Maine, on November 14, 1831, in Bethel. While it is possible that Clement and Susan divorced, such an outcome strikes me as unlikely.

The most notable thing to happen in the prime of Clement's life came in 1839, when still-lingering border issues with British North America

(Canada) came to a head. Such things were supposed to have been settled in the War of 1812, but the occasional skirmish would arise. Maine governor John Fairfield declared "virtual war" on lumberjacks from New Brunswick who were found cutting timber on land owned by Maine. Four regiments of the state militia were mustered in Bangor and marched to the border, but there was no actual fighting—the bluff was enough. The only casualties were two Canadians injured by bears. Clement, who watched his corner of America change around him, died on August 18, 1875.

Porter Clement Seavey was born in July 1845 in Albany, Maine, to Clement and Janet Seavey. He came of age just as the Civil War was taking off. Maine was the first state in the Northeast to support the new antislavery Republican Party, partly due to the influence of evangelical Protestantism. The Seavey family was never known to be political, and which party they preferred (if any) is unknown. Abraham Lincoln chose Maine senator Hannibal Hamlin as his first vice president. Maine was so enthusiastic for the cause of preserving the Union in the war that it ended up contributing a larger number of combatants, in proportion to its population, than any other Union state. Despite being of age when the war was in full swing, no record of Porter enlisting has been found.

According to his obituary, "little is known" of Porter Seavey's early life, though the newspaper claimed he "was employed in the Michigan copper mines and worked at various trades in the western states." His time in Michigan is not reflected in the census, so his time there was brief if the journey ever happened at all.

Porter and Josephine Ward were married by Justice of the Peace Jacob Holt Lovejoy in Albany, Maine, on January 25, 1868, when she was still a teenager. Lovejoy wrote in his diary: "At home; some wind. I worked in the woods some in the forenoon. Afternoon I make two deeds and marry Pastor Seavey to Miss Josephine C. Ward."

The marriage did not last long. Josephine died on October 7, 1872, age twenty, and is buried at Grover Hill Cemetery in Bethel, Maine, near her husband's family. Her death was horrific. As reported in the county newspaper, Josephine "was awaked by the crying of her child, and while lighting a lamp, a bottle of camphor fell from a shelf and was spilt upon her person. The alcohol ignited as soon as she lit the match, and flames spread over her whole person, burning her breast so shockingly."

Porter was a farmer in Albany in 1880. Around 1900 and for the rest of his life, Porter lived in Norway, in Oxford County. Following his move, Porter became a schooner captain. Historian Thomas Edward Jacques cites an Anna Gray (not otherwise identified) as claiming that Porter had at one time been a minister. Such a claim did not seem to have a foundation until a passing mention was found in Lovejoy's diary. Perhaps "Pastor" is merely a poor transcription of "Porter," or perhaps not. No other source identifying him as a pastor of anything is known. Contemporary sources refer to Porter as an independent carpenter who would construct houses and sell them at profit.

Our protagonist, Daniel William Seavey, was allegedly born in Portland, Cumberland County, Maine, on March 23, 1865. Sources such as Dr. Richard Boyd typically use this 1865 birth date, though Boyd believes the birthplace to be Bethel, more in line with where the family lived. This is "allegedly" the date, because it seems unlikely that Daniel was born a full three years prior to his parents' marriage. The 1880 census has Daniel being born circa 1869, which seems more likely and is in line with the marriage date. Also, if Josephine was really only twenty at the time of her death, she would have been only twelve or thirteen in 1865, which is almost unthinkable. A sister, Jennie, was born to Porter and Josephine around 1870, but nothing is known of her childhood.

Porter had remarried to one Alice F. Page on March 26, 1877 (again in Albany, again in front of Justice of the Peace Lovejoy), giving Daniel a stepmother. Lovejoy wrote in his diary: "Cloud in afternoon and evening; quite rainy. In the afternoon, Mr. Porter Seavey and Lady called to be married. I granted their request and made the two as one." This time around, the bride was not even worthy of being named.

Dan allegedly left home at the age of twelve or thirteen and became a sailor aboard tramp schooners and was then serving for a short time in the U.S. Navy around age eighteen. Seavey would later claim he was in the service for about thirty-two months. The math does not add up, but there is a possible solution: if Dan already shifted his birth date from 1869 to 1865 as a teenager, he could have enlisted when he was closer to fifteen or sixteen, a trick that was not unheard of before the days of birth certificates and government identification.

His travels brought him to Peshtigo, Wisconsin, where he settled as much as a traveler ever does. He also worked as a deputy marshal for the Bureau of Indian Affairs in Wisconsin and Minnesota (some sources say Oklahoma and Wisconsin). Jacques merely identifies him as a "government agent" who was out to catch "whiskey smugglers." There is some confusion as to whether Seavey was an agent now or later in life, or both, but now makes more sense, giving him a reason to move west that is otherwise unexplained.

If Peshtigo is known at all today, the town is remembered for the Peshtigo Fire that killed somewhere between 1,200 and 2,500 people in a single day. While the Great Chicago Fire, which happened on the same day, received more press, the Peshtigo blaze remains to this day the deadliest wildfire in history. A full quarter of Peshtigo's citizens perished on that fateful day in 1871, and today, more than 350 of them are located, unidentified, in a mass grave. They were burned so badly that the remains could not be claimed. The tragedy occurred well before Seavey arrived, but not so far before that the trauma was removed from the public consciousness.

In the late 1880s, he moved to nearby Marinette, where he married Mary O. Plumley, who was born in Peshtigo in 1872 and thus was only about fourteen. Mary was the daughter of Horace and Lydia Elizabeth Hollister Plumley. Horace served as a private in Company A in the Wisconsin Thirty-Second Infantry during the Civil War and seems to have been a bit of a wanderer, like his son-in-law. Between 1870 and 1900, Horace moved around the Dairy State repeatedly—from River Falls to Kaukauna to Peshtigo.

While in Marinette County, Boyd says that Seavey "was probably working as a professional trapper." Daughter Harriet was born on August 6, 1889, at Middle Inlet, Marinette County, Wisconsin. And daughter Josephine Orpha was born on September 16, 1890, in Middle Inlet. Boyd lists a daughter named Blanche Violet born in August 1888 and omits Harriet. Blanche and Harriet are, most likely, the same person, as any future reference talks of only two daughters.

Sometime between 1891 and 1895, the Seavey family moved southward to Milwaukee, where Roaring Dan fished, farmed and owned a local saloon downtown. The Milwaukee Business Directory for 1896 confirms that Seavey and partner Charles E. Kenealy operated a tavern at 214 Sycamore Street (later known as West Michigan Street) near the city's harbor. Perhaps visible from their front door were such firms as Gimbel's department store and the Adolph Meinecke Toy Company, both of which had a presence in the area.

A little bit of background on Seavey's new neighborhood is in order. Michigan Street, east of the Milwaukee River, was named by French Canadian fur trader Solomon Juneau and attorney Morgan Lewis Martin in 1837 as part of the Great Lakes–themed Third Ward streets. Others in this scheme were Huron (now Clybourn), Detroit (now St. Paul), Buffalo and Chicago Streets.

Its counterpart, on the west side of the Milwaukee River, was called Sycamore Street in 1835 by government surveyor Byron Kilbourn and his

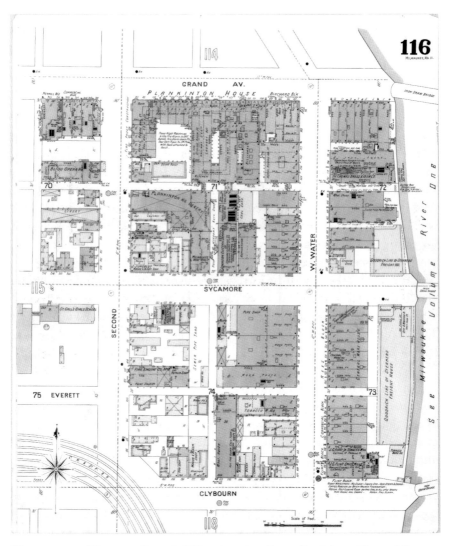

The area around Sycamore Street in Milwaukee when Seavey lived there. *Library of Congress.*

associates. Sycamore was part of the nature-themed streets in Kilbourntown including Spring (Wisconsin), Prairie (Highland), Cedar (Kilbourn), Walnut and Cherry. Kilbourntown merged with the other surrounding neighborhoods on January 31, 1846, to create the core of the Milwaukee we know today; Solomon Juneau was the first mayor.

There were six riots in Milwaukee between 1850 and 1861. The "Bank Riot" was the fifth of these mass protests. The unrest took place on Michigan

A view of Milwaukee in 1901, in the general area of Sycamore. *Library of Congress.*

Street between North Water Street and North Broadway on June 24, 1861, during the opening months of the Civil War.

The riot was inevitable when a state bank association voted to no longer recognize the scrip used for currency by some of its member banks. Several hundred German workers, fearing their money would be worthless, met at North Ninth and West Winnebago Streets that morning. They marched to the banking center on North Water and East Michigan Streets, demanding that their currency retain its value. Prior to a series of National Banking Acts in the 1860s, there was no uniform national currency; one can hardly imagine the confusion of multiple forms of payment, each with its own fluctuating value.

Hundreds of spectators added to the noise and chaos as the mob demonstrated in front of the Fire and Marine Bank, which was headed by railroad executive Alexander Mitchell, said to be the wealthiest man in Wisconsin. When Mitchell came out of his bank to address the crowd, he was greeted by unhappy hoots and hollers. He was forced back into the building when someone threw a paving stone that just missed hitting him.

Then the demonstrators became an out-of-control mob. They attacked the bank, broke open the locked doors and destroyed whatever they could. Bank employees and customers were harassed but escaped without injury. The interior was stripped of its furnishings, which were piled in the street and burned. The State Bank, on the northeast corner of North Water and East Michigan Streets, was the next to receive the mob's wrath, and it suffered the same fate as Mitchell's bank. So did other offices in the building. Their furnishings increased the size of the bonfire. The State Bank building still stands and is now the headquarters of the Grand Avenue Club at 210 East Michigan.

The police force, consisting of a mere eighteen men, was inadequate to keep the rioters in line. Two militia companies were in the city at the time. The Montgomery Guards, a Milwaukee Irish militia, was called to restore order, but because the company was in the process of being sent for training in Madison, there were only thirty-seven members available at the time. They were dispatched to stop the rioters but had no ammunition or bayonets, giving them no real advantage. The rioters backed up as the Guards approached, but the militia's small numbers and lack of weapons soon became apparent to the mob, which began pelting the soldiers with anything they could throw. The company was ordered to retreat while the mob continued its wave of destruction unabated.

When the rioters started a fire to burn the State Bank building, the fire department was called out. It set up its fire engine and aimed its water first at the fire and then at the demonstrators. The rioters scattered when another company of infantrymen, the so-called Zouaves, was called in and charged the mob with bayonets flashing. Later reinforcements of several more militia companies stationed at training camps in Milwaukee brought calm to the city.

The banks were back in business in a few days, and the rioters got what they wanted; the banking association reversed course and promised to recognize their currency.

In the late 1880s, a streetcar controversy was in the news. The plan called for a streetcar line between two railroad stations. The new Union Depot had recently been constructed south of what is now Zeidler Union Square between North Third and North Fourth Streets, and there was hope that the track would be linked with the Chicago and Northwestern Depot at the lake between Michigan and Wisconsin Streets. The line would also connect to a water transportation company at Michigan Street and the river.

The problem was that there was no bridge over the river between Michigan and Sycamore Streets. The bridge was opposed by several aldermen, who complained the money should be spent in their wards. Proponents said the bridge and streetcar line would spur business development, improve transportation and increase property values. Opponents temporarily slowed the construction by taking the matter to court, but the bridge opened in 1891. The streetcar line followed soon after. As expected, new buildings, businesses and housing developed along the street but, due to the Financial Panic of 1893, not as quickly as hoped.

This brings us back up to the time of Dan Seavey and Charles Kenealy, who benefited from the new bridge and streetcar. Trying to identify Kenealy without more context is a challenge, but he may have been the Charles Kenealy (1872–1919) who lived in Milwaukee's Fourth Ward with his parents. A Charles Kenealy also served as a corporal in the Spanish-American War, which would be roughly the right age and time frame. In all likelihood, these two were the same man.

Saloon ownership is likely how Seavey became acquainted with Frederick Pabst (1836–1904), the Milwaukee beer magnate. For many years, bars were often "tied houses," meaning that they served only one brand of beer and that brand's brewery would have a full or partial stake in the business. We do not know for sure, but it is quite possible that Seavey's tavern was a tied house for the Pabst brewery.

Pabst had immigrated with his parents to the United States, settling first in Milwaukee and then Chicago. The following year, his mother died in a cholera epidemic. In Chicago, Frederick and his father had to eke out a living. For a while, they worked as waiters and busboys. Frederick soon gave this up, however, in exchange for adventure. Because he had enjoyed his voyage to America, he decided to become a cabin boy on a Lake Michigan steamer. By the time he was twenty-one, Pabst had earned what was then called a "pilot's license" and was captain of one of these vessels. In this capacity, he met Phillip Best, the owner of a small but prosperous brewery founded by his father, Jacob Best, in 1844 in Milwaukee. Pabst married Best's daughter Maria on March 25, 1862.

For the next year and a half, Pabst continued to ply the waters of Lake Michigan as a ship's captain, until an accident in December 1863 led to a change in career. While trying to bring his craft into Milwaukee harbor, Pabst's ship ran aground. A short while later, Pabst purchased half of Best's brewing company. From this point on, Pabst became the man we remember him for today.

2

THE GOLD RUSH

At this point in our story, we have followed the Seavey family from England west to the New World, becoming pioneers in New Hampshire. Our featured family member, Dan Seavey, became a pioneer in his own right, settling in Milwaukee during its formative years.

Despite a directory placing Seavey in Milwaukee in 1895, by the first half of 1896 he pops up in Portland, Maine again, always a man on the move. In May he was caught passing a counterfeit silver dollar at a grocery store, and "his manner of doing this" made the grocer believe Seavey's was knowingly doing so and not simply someone innocently in possession of such an item. Seavey, who was making a living in town selling door plates, swore to Deputy Marshal Hartnett that he acquired the dollar from a man who gave him change for a five. Seavey was unable to describe the man.

A search of Seavey's apartment on Vine Street found a counterfeiting laboratory with aluminum, other white metals, a mould for forming coins and plaster of paris for creating the moulds. Even when confronted with the evidence, Seavey denied he was a counterfeiter and now said he would sometimes make "tokens." The newspapers believed he was a poor man, as he seemingly had no furniture and very little to eat, as well as sharing his small quarters with his recently divorced sister Jennie Thompson (or, alternatively, Thomas).

Interest soon turned from the counterfeiting allegations to what was deemed "something rather peculiar" about Seavey and his sister. The *Portland Daily Press* noted, "They have been living in one room and to every appearance like man and wife. Their manner toward each other is not at all like that of brother and sister." The *Boston Herald* picked up the story, saying that the pair had not grown up together and met by sheer chance in Milwaukee, before returning to Maine in February. Upon meeting as adults, "an infatuation ... took possession of them." At first, "they boarded for a time at the home of a cousin, but she took exceptions to the nature of their attention toward each other, and ordered them to find a boarding place elsewhere." Seavey refused to comment other than to say it was all slander.

I have been unable to find the outcome of Seavey's trial through the newspaper record, but the timeline suggests he was acquitted. Perhaps he was merely asked to leave the state, because the next stage of Seavey's story takes place as far from Maine and into the final frontier as one could get, excluding outer space. Some background is in order.

The Russians and the fur-trading Hudson's Bay Company of Canada had both explored the Yukon in the first half of the nineteenth century but ignored the rumors of gold in favor of fur trading. A tried and true business, it offered more immediate profits while beaver was king. In fact,

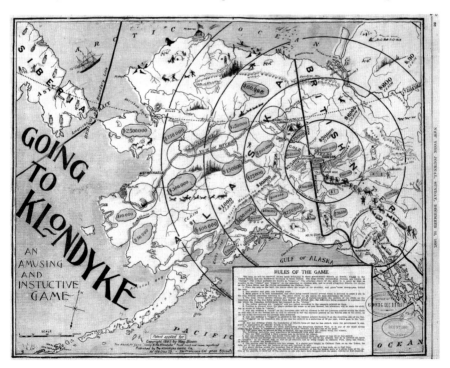

A humorous map/game in circulation at the time of the Klondike Gold Rush. *Library of Congress*.

some of the first prospectors had to supplement their income with fur trading in order to survive.

In the second half of the nineteenth century, however, American prospectors began to spread into the area. The United States had purchased Alaska from the Russians in 1867. Which party received the better deal is hard to say, though it would soon tip in the Americans' favor. Making deals with the native tribes, the early prospectors opened the important routes of Chilkoot and White Pass and trickled into the Yukon Valley between 1870 and 1890.

Here, they encountered the native Han people, seminomadic hunters and fishermen who lived along the Yukon and Klondike Rivers. The Han did not appear to know about the vast amount of gold deposits in the region, or perhaps such things were simply of no interest to them. One member of the Han later commented that "my people knew all the Klondike, but they never know nothing about gold." Other native groups included the Tlingit and the Tagish. The former still exist in the region today, while the Tagish have essentially disappeared through intermarriage. The last speaker of their language passed in 2008.

In 1883, Indian scout Edward Lawrence Schieffelin identified gold deposits along the Yukon River. Schieffelin must have been blessed with incredible luck, as he had previously been the one to discover silver in Arizona and launched the founding of Tombstone. Despite finding gold, he did not live to see the rush he started. An expedition up the Fortymile River in 1886 discovered considerable amounts of gold deposits and led to the founding of Fortymile City. That same year, gold had been found on the banks of the Klondike River, but in smaller amounts, and no claims were made. By the late 1880s, several hundred miners were working their way along the Yukon Valley, living in small mining camps and trading with the Han. On the Alaskan side of the border with Canada, Circle City, a logging town, was established in 1893 on the Yukon River. In three years, Circle City grew to become the hyperbolic "Paris of Alaska," with twelve hundred inhabitants utilizing saloons, opera houses, schools and libraries. In 1896, the boomtown was so well known that a journalist from the *Chicago Daily Record* came to visit. Yet, at the end of the year, Circle City became a ghost town almost overnight when large gold deposits were found upstream on the Klondike.

On August 16, 1896, an American trapper-turned-prospector named George Washington Carmack; his Tagish wife, Kate; her brother Keish (more commonly known as "Skookum Jim" Mason); and their nephew

Dawson Charlie were traveling south of the Klondike River. Following a suggestion from Robert Henderson, a Nova Scotian prospector, they began looking for gold on Bonanza Creek (called Rabbit Creek before the "bonanza"), one of the Klondike's tributaries. Today, there is no way to know who actually discovered the gold, George Carmack or Skookum Jim, but the group agreed to let Carmack appear as the official discoverer, as they feared that authorities would not recognize an indigenous claimant. Henderson was also known to be prejudiced against the natives and may have objected or even challenged the claim. Although he never became rich from gold, Henderson was later pensioned $200 per month by the Canadian government as a "thank you" for helping launch the stampede.

In any event, gold was present along the river in huge quantities. Carmack measured out four claims, strips of ground that could later be legally mined by the owner, along the river. These included two for himself—one as his normal claim, the second as a reward for having discovered the gold—and one each for Jim and Charlie. The claims were registered the next day at the police post at the mouth of the Fortymile River. News of their success spread rapidly from there to other mining camps in the Yukon River valley.

By the end of August, all of Bonanza Creek had been claimed by miners. A Slovenian prospector named Anton Stander, short on options, advanced up into one of the creeks feeding into Bonanza, later to be named Eldorado Creek. He discovered new sources of gold there, which would prove to be even richer than those on Bonanza. Unproven claims began to be sold between miners and speculators for considerable sums. Just before Christmas, word of the gold reached Circle City. Despite the obstacles of winter, many prospectors immediately left for the Klondike by dogsled, eager to reach the region before the best claims were taken. The outside world was still largely unaware of the news and although Canadian officials, including government surveyor William Ogilvie (an acquaintance of Skookum Jim), had managed to send a message to their superiors in Ottawa in January about the finds and influx of prospectors, the government did not give the news much attention. The winter prevented river traffic, and it was not until June 1897 that the first boats left the area, carrying the freshly mined gold and the full story of the discoveries.

In the resulting Klondike stampede, an estimated one hundred thousand people tried to reach the Klondike goldfields, but because of the difficulties, only around thirty thousand to forty thousand eventually did. The broad estimated numbers involved in the stampede are derived from the law enforcement statistics generated along the trails. This initial influx formed the height of the Klondike Gold Rush from the summer of 1897 until the summer of 1898.

The stampede began on July 15, 1897, in San Francisco and was spurred on two days later in Seattle, when the first of the early prospectors returned from the Klondike, bringing with them large amounts of gold on the ships *Excelsior* and *Portland*. The press reported that a total of $1,139,000 had been brought in by these ships, an astonishing amount for the time. In fact, this turned out to be an underestimate. The migration of prospectors north that same week caught so much attention that the would-be miners were joined by outfitters, writers and photographers. Unknown to all of those hopefuls, the best claims were staked by the time the *Excelsior* reached the port.

Various factors lay behind this sudden mass response. Economically, the news had reached the United States at the height of a series of financial recessions and bank failures in the 1890s. The gold standard of the time had paper money backed by the production of gold, and shortages toward the end of the nineteenth century meant that gold dollars were rapidly increasing in value ahead of paper currencies and were being hoarded. This had contributed to the Panics of 1893 and 1896, which caused unemployment and financial uncertainty. There was a huge, unresolved demand for gold across the developed world that the Klondike promised to fulfill. And, for individuals, the region promised higher wages or maybe even financial security.

The Klondike, as described by historian Pierre Berton, was "just far enough away to be romantic and just close enough to be accessible." Furthermore, the Pacific ports closest to the gold strikes were desperate to encourage trade and travel to the region. The mass journalism of the period promoted the event and the human-interest stories that lay behind this sudden migration. A worldwide publicity campaign engineered largely by Erastus Brainerd, the editor of the *Seattle Press*, helped establish that city as the premier supply center and the departure point for the gold fields. Seattle had previously experienced a boom as a lumber town, but it was in a slump. The rush would change the city forever.

Seattle and San Francisco competed fiercely for business during the rush, with Seattle winning the larger share of trade, perhaps due to its proximity, but more likely from the tireless promotion of Brainerd. Indeed, one of the first to join the gold rush was William D. Wood, the mayor of Seattle, who resigned and formed a company to transport prospectors to the Klondike. He went north on August 16. His company had to spend the winter along the frozen Yukon River, eating the supplies that Wood had hoped to sell at a profit in Dawson. Now he was forced to sell at his purchase price.

The prospectors came from many nations, although an estimated 60 to 80 percent were native-born Americans like Dan Seavey or recent immigrants to America. The 1898 census shows that 63 percent of Dawson City residents at the time were American citizens; 32 percent were British (including Canadians). Most had no experience in the mining industry, being white-collar clerks or salesmen rather than hardy laborers. Mass resignations of staff to join the gold rush became notorious. In Seattle, this included not only Mayor Wood but also twelve policemen and a significant percentage of the city's streetcar drivers.

Some stampeders were famous in their day: John McGraw, the former governor of Washington—best recalled for his time in Seattle during the anti-Chinese riots—went up the coast with a prominent lawyer friend. American scout and explorer Frederick Russell Burnham arrived from Africa with his twelve-year-old son, only to leave as soon as the Spanish-American War started. He missed that conflict but took part in the Second Boer War the following year. Among those who documented the rush were the Swedish photographer Eric A. Hegg, who took some of the iconic pictures of Chilkoot Pass, and photojournalist Tappan Adney, who afterward wrote a firsthand history of the stampede, *The Klondike Stampede* (1900). Jack London, later a famous novelist, left to seek his fortune but made his money during the rush mostly by working for prospectors. For example, he worked as a river pilot on the rapids of Whitehorse in the summer of 1898.

The publicity around the gold rush led to a flurry of branded goods being put on the market, all sold as "Klondike" goods, allegedly designed for the Northwest. The range of Klondike-themed products was huge, from special food to glasses, boots, cigars, medicines, soup, blankets and stoves. The selection included some unusual offers such as a special Klondike bicycle, "ice bicycles," a wind-powered "boat sled," a "snow train," clockwork gold pans and an X-ray gold detector designed by none other than Nikola Tesla. Guidebooks were published, giving advice about routes, equipment, mining and funding necessary for the enterprise. Contemporary newspapers referred to this phenomenon as "Klondicitis."

The Klondike could be reached only by the Yukon River, either upstream from its mouth in the Bering Sea, downstream from its source at Atlin Lake or from somewhere in the middle through its tributaries. Riverboats could navigate the Yukon in the summer from the delta until a point called Whitehorse, above the Klondike. Travel in general was made difficult by both the geography and the climate. The region was mountainous, and the rivers were winding and sometimes impassable. The short summers could be surprisingly hot, while from October to June, during the long winters, temperatures could drop below minus fifty-eight degrees Fahrenheit. If the cold wasn't enough to kill, the frostbite was guaranteed to cost the unprepared a few fingers and toes.

The weather could be both a help and an obstacle. Winter travel meant deep snow and treacherous ice. However, the mud that formed each spring and fall would be frozen, and snow would cover the sharp, jagged rocks that the traveler would have to avoid in the summer. In theory, it was possible to travel even during winter using teams of dogs, but if the temperature dropped significantly, even dogsled teams would have to rest and take shelter. Aids for the travelers to carry their supplies varied. Some had brought dogs, horses, mules or oxen; others had to rely on carrying their equipment on their backs or on sleds pulled by hand. Shortly after the stampede began in 1897, the Canadian authorities introduced rules requiring anyone entering Yukon Territory to bring with them a year's supply of food; typically, this weighed around 1,150 pounds. While this may sound excessive, the rationale was quite reasonable: the government did not wish to spend an inordinate amount of time rescuing starving foreigners. By the time camping equipment, tools and other essentials were included, a typical traveler was transporting as much as a ton in weight. Unsurprisingly, the price of pack animals soared. At the port city of Dyea, even poor-quality horses could sell for as much as $700 or be rented out for $40 a day. Before the rush, the price of such animals was a mere $4.

From Seattle or San Francisco, prospectors could travel by sea up the coast to the Alaskan ports of Dyea and Skagway. The coastal route is now referred to as the Inside Passage. The sudden increase in demand encouraged a range of vessels to be used for transportation, including old paddle wheelers, fishing boats, barges and coal ships still full of coal dust. All were overloaded, and many sank.

To sail all the way to the Klondike was possible, first from Seattle across the northern Pacific to the Alaskan coast. From St. Michael, at the Yukon River delta, a riverboat could then take the prospectors the rest of the way up the river to Dawson, often guided by one of the native Koyukon people who lived near St. Michael. Although this all-water route, also called "the rich man's route," was expensive and long—4,700 miles in total—it had the attraction of greater speed and avoiding the pitfalls of overland travel. At the beginning of the stampede, a ticket could be bought for $150, while during the winter of 1897–98, the fare settled at $1,000. On the other hand, competition among railways to attract Klondikers ultimately led to a reduction in train fares.

In 1897, some eighteen hundred travelers attempted the all-water route, but the vast majority were caught along the river when the Yukon iced over in October. Only forty-three reached the Klondike before winter, and of those, thirty-five had to return, having thrown away their equipment on the way to reach their destination in time. The remainder mostly found themselves stranded in isolated camps and settlements along the ice-covered river, often in desperate circumstances.

Most of the prospectors landed at the southeast Alaskan towns of Dyea and Skagway, both located at the entrance of the natural Lynn Canal at the end of the Inside Passage. From there, they needed to travel over the mountain ranges into Canada's Yukon Territory and then down the river network to the Klondike. Along the trails, tent camps sprang up at places where prospectors had to stop to eat or sleep or at obstacles such as the icy lakes at the head of the Yukon. At the start of the rush, a ticket from Seattle to the port of Dyea cost $40 for a ship cabin. Premiums of $100, however, were soon paid, and the steamship companies hesitated to post their rates in advance, since they could increase on a daily basis.

Those who landed at Skagway made their way over the White Pass before cutting across to Bennett Lake. Although the trail began gently, the route progressed over several mountains with paths as narrow as two feet and in wider parts covered with boulders and sharp rocks. Under these conditions, horses died in huge numbers. Jack London wrote of the horses: "Men shot them, worked them to death and when they were gone, went back to the beach and bought more.…Their hearts turned to stone—those which did not break—and they became beasts, the men on the Dead Horse Trail." This was the informal name many gave to the White Pass, for obvious reasons. The volume of travelers and the wet weather made the trail impassable, and by late 1897, the route was closed until further notice, leaving around five thousand eager men stranded in Skagway.

An alternative toll road suitable for wagons was eventually constructed, and this, combined with colder weather that froze the muddy ground, allowed the White Pass to reopen. Prospectors began to make their way into Canada. Moving supplies and equipment over the pass had to be done in stages. Most travelers divided their belongings into sixty-five-pound packages that could be carried on a man's back or heavier loads that could be pulled by hand on a sled. Carrying packages forward and walking back for more, a prospector would need about thirty round trips, a distance of at least twenty-five hundred miles, before they had moved all of their supplies to the end of the trail. Even using a heavy sled, a strong man would be covering one thousand miles and need around ninety days to reach Lake Bennett.

Those who landed at Dyea traveled the Chilkoot Trail and crossed its pass to reach Lake Lindeman, which fed into Lake Bennett at the head of the Yukon River. The Chilkoot Pass was higher than the White Pass, but more men chose the former option: around twenty-two thousand during the gold rush. The trail passed up through camps until it reached a flat ledge, just before the main ascent, which was too steep for animals. Horses abandoned before the summit were later rounded up and shot. This location, known as the Scales, was where goods were weighed before travelers officially entered Canada. The cold, the steepness and the weight of equipment made the climb extremely onerous, and it could take a full day to get to the top of the one-thousand-foot-high slope.

As on the White Pass trail, supplies needed to be broken down into smaller packages and carried in relay. Packers, prepared to carry supplies for cash, were available along the route but would charge up to one dollar per pound on the later stages. Many of these packers were natives—Tlingits or Tagish. Avalanches were common in the mountains, and, on April 3, 1898, one claimed the lives of more than sixty people traveling over Chilkoot Pass. Approximately seventy people were initially believed to have been buried by the snow, including between six and nine people subsequently rescued. However, without knowing everyone who was in the area, the final toll remains uncertain. Bodies may still be there today.

Entrepreneurs began to provide solutions as the winter progressed. Steps were cut into the ice at the Chilkoot Pass that could be used for a daily fee. This fifteen-hundred-step staircase became known as the "Golden Steps." By December 1897, one Archie Burns built a railway up the final parts of the Chilkoot Pass, from the Scales to the false summit. A horse at the bottom turned a wheel, which pulled a rope running to the top and back; freight was loaded on sledges pulled by the rope. Five more railways soon followed, one powered by a steam engine, charging between eight and thirty cents per pound. An aerial railway built in the spring of 1898 was able to move nine tons of goods an hour up to the summit.

At Lakes Bennett and Lindeman, the prospectors stopped to build rafts or boats that would take them the final five hundred miles down the Yukon to Dawson City in the spring. Some craft were hauled over the passes whole or piecemeal. One was the sternwheeler *A.J. Goddard*, a small riverboat transported in pieces to Lake Bennett and assembled there. After all that trouble, it made only one trip to Dawson. In May 1898, 7,124 boats of varying sizes and qualities left. By that time, the forests around the lakes had been largely cut down for timber, but the river posed a new problem. Above Whitehorse, the river was dangerous, with several rapids along the Miles Canyon through to the White Horse Rapids.

After many boats were wrecked and several hundred people died, the Northwest Mounted Police (NWMP, now the Royal Canadian Mounted Police, or RCMP) introduced safety rules, inspecting the boats carefully and forbidding women and children to travel through the rapids. Additional rules stated that any boat carrying passengers required a licensed ship captain, typically costing twenty-five dollars, although some prospectors simply unpacked their boats and let them drift unmanned through the rapids with the intent of walking down to collect them on the other side. During the summer, a horse-pulled streetcar track, capable of carrying boats and equipment through the canyon at twenty-five dollars a time, removed the need for prospectors to navigate the rapids.

There were a few more trails established during 1898 from southeast Alaska to the Yukon River. One was the Dalton trail: starting from Dyea, the trail went across the Chilkat Pass west of Chilkoot and turned north to the Yukon River at Fort Selkirk, a distance of about 350 miles. This was created by cowboy cartographer Jack Dalton as a summer route, intended for cattle and horses, and Dalton charged a toll of $250 for its use. Toll roads were an interesting part of the journey. George Brackett made his trail and charged for passage but ended up losing more than he gained because of the legal fees for suing trespassers. Dalton turned a profit thanks to his secret weapon—rather than lawsuits, he carried a shotgun.

The Takou route started from Juneau and went northeast to Teslin Lake. From here, the path followed a river to the Yukon, where it met the Dyea and Skagway route at a point halfway to the Klondike. Choosing this way meant dragging and poling canoes upriver and through mud, together with crossing a five-thousand-foot mountain along a narrow trail. Finally, there was the Stikine route starting from the port of Wrangell farther southeast of Skagway. This route went up the uneasy Stikine River to Glenora, the head of navigation. From Glenora, prospectors would have to carry their supplies 150 miles to Teslin Lake, where it, like the Takou route, met the Yukon River system.

An alternative to the southeast Alaskan ports were the "All-Canadian" routes, so called because they mostly stayed on Canadian soil throughout their journey. These were popular with Canadians for patriotic reasons and because they avoided American customs. The first of these, about one thousand miles in length, started from Ashcroft in British Columbia and crossed swamps, river gorges and mountains until the route met with the Stikine River route at Glenora. By international treaty, Canadians had the right of free navigation along the Stikine River and therefore counted it as an All-Canadian route. From Glenora, prospectors would face the same difficulties as those who came from Wrangell. At least fifteen hundred men attempted to travel along the Ashcroft route and five thousand along the Stikine. The mud and the slushy ice of the two routes proved exhausting, killing or incapacitating the pack animals and creating chaos among the travelers.

Three more routes started from Edmonton, Alberta. These were not much better—barely trails at all—despite being advertised as "the inside track" and the "back door to the Klondike." One, the "overland route," headed northwest from Edmonton, ultimately meeting the Peace River and then continuing overland to the Klondike, crossing the Liard River on the way. To encourage travel via Edmonton, the government hired road engineer Thomas W. Chalmers to clear a trail through the woods, which became known as the Klondike Trail. The other two trails, known as the "water routes," involved more river travel. One went by boat along rivers and overland to the Yukon River system at Pelly River and from there to Dawson. Another went north of Dawson by the Mackenzie River to Fort McPherson before entering Alaska and meeting the Yukon River at Fort Yukon, downstream to the Klondike. From here, the boat and equipment had to be pulled up the Yukon about four hundred miles. An estimated 1,660 travelers took these three routes, of whom only 685 arrived, some taking up to eighteen months to make the journey.

An equivalent to the All-Canadian routes was the "All-American route," which aimed to reach the Yukon from the port of Valdez, which lay farther along the Alaskan coast from Skagway. This, it was hoped, would evade the Canadian customs posts and provide an American-controlled route into the interior. From late 1897 onward, thirty-five hundred men and women attempted the route; delayed by the winter snows, fresh efforts were made in the spring.

In practice, the huge Valdez Glacier that stood between the port and the Alaskan interior was almost impassable, and only two hundred people managed to pass this point. By 1899, the cold and scurvy was causing many deaths among the rest. Other prospectors attempted an alternative route across the Malaspina Glacier just to the east, suffering even greater setbacks. Those who did manage to cross the latter glacier found themselves fighting their way through miles of wilderness before they could reach Dawson. Their expedition was forced to turn back the same way they had come, with only four men surviving.

The border of southeast Alaska had been disputed between the United States and Canada ever since the Americans acquired the land from Russia in 1867. The States and Canada both claimed the ports of Dyea and Skagway. This, combined with the number of American prospectors, the quantities of gold being mined and the difficulties in exercising government authority in such a remote area, made control of the border a sensitive diplomatic issue.

Early in the gold rush, the U.S. Army sent a small contingent to Circle City in case intervention was required in the Klondike, while the Canadian government considered excluding all American prospectors from the Yukon altogether. Neither took place; instead, the United States agreed to make Dyea an acceptable port of entry for Canadians, allowing British ships to bring Canadian passengers and goods there, while Canada agreed to permit American miners to operate in the Klondike. Today, Dyea is considered a "former town," with its few remnants absorbed into Skagway.

The Northwest Mounted Police set up control posts at the borders of the Yukon Territory or, where that was disputed, at easily controlled points such as the Chilkoot and White Passes. These units were armed with Maxim machine guns. Their tasks included enforcing the rules requiring that travelers bring a year's supply of food with them to be allowed into the Yukon Territory (as mentioned earlier), checking for illegal weapons, preventing the entry of criminals and enforcing customs duties.

This last task was particularly unpopular with American prospectors, who faced paying an average of 25 percent of the value of their goods and supplies. The Mounties had a reputation for running these posts honestly, although accusations were made that some of them took bribes. Prospectors, on the other hand, tried to smuggle prized items like silk and whiskey across the pass in tins and bales of hay: the former item for the ladies, the latter for the saloons.

The stampede had already been going on for a while by the time the gold fever reached Milwaukee. In 1898, Seavey left his family in Milwaukee to participate in the Klondike Gold Rush. If his partner Charles Kenealy is the same Kenealy who was serving in the Spanish-American War, this would make sense as a logical time for Seavey to leave the tavern business. Allegedly, he joined Captain Frederick Pabst in this business venture after selling his

Milwaukee property (which included vast farmland) for an impressive $14,000 and buying 10 percent of Pabst's Rosebud Mining Company. As Seavey would later explain, ten men each owned 10 percent, though the only other man named publicly was Louis Auer. Unfortunately, any record of the Rosebud Mining Company has not been found; future historians may uncover the remaining seven names.

Auer had a very successful insurance and real estate business that he inherited when his father passed. He was later a general in the Wisconsin National Guard and a member of the Milwaukee Park Commission. Along with President Theodore Roosevelt and many others of the era, Auer accepted a racist interpretation of eugenics. Auer was afraid that Germans and Englishmen (those of the best genes) were eventually going to lose their grip on the country due to so-called race suicide. As the number of children born to English descendants declined, they would eventually die out. Meanwhile, there was the massive increase in immigration to the United States. The incoming Italians, Poles, Slovaks, Hungarians and others were considered people with lesser genes, and the fear was that they would outnumber those who had "better" genes. These newcomers were mostly Catholics and did not use birth control, resulting in larger families that would exacerbate the increase.

Years after his time with Seavey, Auer devised a plan to "fix" this problem of racial imbalance. He built apartments in what was then a German neighborhood. The apartment floors were soundproof so that neighbors would not complain of children making too much noise. The complex included courtyards and playgrounds for the children, and Auer advertised his desire to rent to ("genetically appropriate") families. He also promised free rent during the month a baby was born in one of his flats, earning him the title of "Baby Flat Landlord." In the first year, Auer had given seven months' free rent for the seven babies born in his nearly two-hundred-apartment complex.

Auer was so pleased with the results that he decided he could do even more by playing matchmaker. He announced plans to increase the birth rate even more by building a huge apartment that would help to promote matrimony among those of the proper "racial" background. The apartments in one wing would be rented to bachelors and the other wing to what he called "bachelor maids." The wings would be separated by apartments occupied by married couples, who would act as chaperones to prevent any mingling in the singles' wings. Auer hoped that marriages would ensue, and he promised that he would give a month's free rent to any couple from his building who

BRIGADIER-GENERAL LOUIS AUER.

QUARTERMASTER AND COMMISSARY-GENERAL.

Louis Auer, a promoter of eugenics and one of the Milwaukee men who funded the Rosebud Mining Company. *Wikicommons.*

tied the knot. To make a long story short, this concept did not outlive Auer and has rightly been forgotten.

Seavey was sent to Alaska with "Twilger and Company," which had the contract to perform tests for Rosebud. No record of "Twilger" has been found, making it as much of a mystery as Rosebud. Perhaps the newspapers misquoted Seavey and he was referring to Fred Terwilliger, a noted prospector. Certainly funding someone who already knows the proper methods would make sense. We do not know which route Seavey took—possibly water, more likely the All-American—but he apparently made it to Dawson City.

Of the estimated 30,000 to 40,000 people who reached Dawson City during the gold rush, only around 15,000 to 20,000 finally became prospectors. Of these, no more than 4,000 struck gold, and only a few hundred became rich. By the time most of the stampeders arrived in 1898, the best creeks had all been claimed, either by the long-term miners in the region or by the first arrivals of the year before. The Bonanza, Eldorado, Hunker and Dominion Creeks were all taken, with almost ten thousand claims recorded by the authorities by July 1898; a new prospector such as Seavey would have to look farther afield to find a claim of his own.

Geologically, the region was permeated with veins of gold, brought to the surface by volcanic action and then worn away by the erosion of rivers and streams, leaving nuggets and gold dust in deposits known as placer gold. Often, gold will be left in uneroded ores called mother lodes; however, at Klondike, a mother lode has never been found. Some ores lay along the creek beds, typically fifteen to thirty feet beneath the surface. Others, formed by even older streams, lay along the hilltops; these deposits were called "bench gold." Finding the gold was a challenge. Initially, miners had assumed that all the gold would be along the existing creeks, and it was not until late in 1897 that the hilltops began to be mined. Gold was also unevenly distributed in the areas where the nuggets were found, which made the prediction of good mining sites even more unreliable. The only way to be certain that gold was present was to conduct exploratory digging.

Mining began with clearing the ground of vegetation and debris. Prospect holes were then dug in an attempt to find the ore or "pay streak." If these holes looked productive, proper digging could commence, aiming down to the bedrock, where the majority of the gold was found. The digging would be carefully monitored in case the operation needed to be shifted to allow for changes in the flow.

In the frozen climate of the Klondike, a layer of hard permafrost lay only six feet below the surface. Traditionally, this had meant that mining in the region occurred only during the summer months, but the pressure of the gold rush made such a delay unacceptable. In the late nineteenth century, technology existed for dealing with this problem, including hydraulic mining and stripping, and dredging, but the heavy equipment required for this could not be brought into the Klondike during the gold rush. Bringing food and other supplies was challenging enough.

Instead, the miners relied on wood fires to soften the ground to a depth of about fourteen inches and then removing the gravel. The process was repeated until the gold was reached, if any existed. In theory, no support of the shaft was necessary because of the permafrost; in practice, the fire sometimes melted the permafrost and caused collapses. Fires could also produce noxious gases, which had to be removed by bellows or other tools. The resulting "dirt" brought out of the mines froze quickly in winter and could be processed only during the warmer summer months. In the summer, the sunshine would slowly thaw exposed permafrost at the rate of about two feet every twelve hours; some miners felt this was too slow and used burning techniques during the summer months as well. An alternative, more efficient approach called steam thawing was devised between 1897 and 1898; this used a furnace to pump steam directly into the ground. But since this method required additional equipment, it was not a widespread technique during the few years of the rush.

In the summer, water would be used to sluice and pan the dirt, separating out the heavier gold from gravel. This required miners to construct sluices, which were sequences of wood boxes fifteen feet long through which the dirt was washed; up to twenty of these might be needed for each mining operation. The sluices in turn required lots of water, usually produced by creating a dam and ditches or crude pipes. "Bench gold" mining on the hillsides could not use sluice lines, because water could not be pumped that high up. Instead, these mines used rockers, boxes that moved back and forth like a cradle, to create the motion needed for separation. Finally, the resulting gold dust could be exported out of the Klondike. The product was then either exchanged for paper money at the rate of sixteen dollars per ounce through one of the major banks that opened in Dawson City or simply used as money when dealing with local traders. "Commercial dust," still containing some black sand, was bought by banks at the reduced rate of eleven dollars per ounce. Local traders often accepted commercial dust at the pure dust rate but made up for this by under-weighing.

Successful mining took time and capital, particularly once most of the timber around the Klondike had been cut down. A realistic mining operation required $1,500 for wood to be burned to melt the ground, along with about $1,000 to construct a dam, $1,500 for ditches and up to $600 for sluice boxes—a total of $4,600. The attraction of the Klondike to a prospector, however, was that when gold was found, the ore was often highly concentrated. Some of the creeks in the Klondike were fifteen times richer in gold than those claimed in California fifty years earlier, and richer still than those in South Africa. In just two years, for example, $230,000 worth of gold was brought up from claim no. 29 on the Eldorado Creek. The claim belonged to miner Charlie Anderson, known as the "Lucky Swede." He had bought the land unproved while too drunk to remember. The next morning, Anderson disputed the purchase, but the contract was enforced by the NWMP. Luckily for him, the blind buy proved to be incredibly profitable.

Under Canadian law, miners first had to get a license, either when they arrived at Dawson or on the way from Victoria in British Columbia. They could then prospect for gold and, when they had found a suitable location, lay claim to mining rights over said gold. To "stake" a claim, a prospector would literally drive stakes into the ground a measured distance apart and then return to Dawson to register the claim for fifteen dollars. This normally had to be done within three days. By 1897, only one claim per person at a time was allowed in a district, although married couples could exploit a loophole that allowed a wife to register a claim in her own name, doubling their amount of land.

The claim could be mined freely for a year, after which a $100 fee had to be paid annually. Should the prospector leave the claim for more than three days without good reason, it was considered abandoned and another miner could make a claim on the land. Beginning in September 1897, the Canadian government also charged a royalty of between 10 and 20 percent on the value of gold taken from a claim.

Traditionally, a mining claim had been granted over a 500-foot-long stretch of a creek, including the land from one side of the valley to another. The Canadian authorities had tried to reduce this length to 150 feet in order to sell more claims but under pressure from miners had been forced to compromise at 250 feet. The only exception to this was a "discovery" claim, the first to be made on a creek, which could be the full 500 feet long. Despite the tensions over the sizes of claims in the Klondike, the position of miners was in fact more secure than it had been in the California Gold Rush of 1848–52, where an influx of prospectors could lead to a reduction in size of existing claims. The exact lengths of claims were often challenged, and when government surveyor William Ogilvie (previously mentioned) conducted surveys to settle disputes, he found that some claims exceeded the official limit. The excess fractions of land, often as small as a few feet, then became available as claims in themselves and were sometimes quite valuable.

Claims could also be bought from other miners. However, their price depended on whether they had been proved to contain gold. A prospector with capital might consider taking a risk on an "unproved" claim on one of the better yielding creeks for $5,000; a wealthier miner could buy a "proved" mine for $50,000. The well-known claim no. 8 on Eldorado Creek was sold for as much as $350,000. Prospectors were also allowed to hire others to work for them. Enterprising miners such as Alex McDonald (who had previously mined copper in Colorado) set about collecting mines and employees, earning him the nickname "King of the Klondike." McDonald would expand his acquisitions with short-term loans and, by the autumn of 1897, had purchased twenty-eight claims, estimated to be worth millions. Early on, he was estimated to be making $5,000 a day in gold. One brilliant investment was a building in Dawson that McDonald rented out to the federal government for use as a post office. "Swiftwater" Bill Gates famously borrowed heavily against his claim on the Eldorado Creek, relying on hired hands to mine the gold to keep up his interest payments.

The less fortunate or less well funded prospectors rapidly found themselves destitute. Some chose to sell their equipment and return south. Others took jobs as manual workers, either in mines or in Dawson; the typical daily pay of fifteen dollars was high by the contemporary standards of Canada and the lower 48 but low compared to the cost of living in the Klondike. The possibility that a new creek might suddenly produce gold, however, continued to tempt poorer prospectors. Smaller stampedes around the Klondike continued throughout the gold rush, when rumors of new strikes would cause a small mob to descend on fresh sites hoping to be able to stake out a high-value claim.

The massive influx of prospectors drove the formation of boomtowns along the routes of the stampede, with Dawson City in the Klondike the largest. The new towns were crowded, often chaotic, and many disappeared just as soon as they came. Most stampeders were men, but women also traveled to the region, typically as wives of prospectors. Some women entertained in gambling dens and dance halls built by business owners who were encouraged by the lavish spending of successful miners.

Dawson remained relatively lawful, protected by the Canadian NWMP, which meant that vices such as gambling and prostitution were accepted while the more serious crimes of robbery and murder were kept low. By contrast, the port of Skagway in southeast Alaska became infamous for its criminal underworld. The extreme climate and remoteness of the region in general meant that supplies and communication with the outside world, including news and mail were scarce.

The ports of Dyea and Skagway, through which most of the prospectors entered, were tiny settlements before the gold rush, each consisting of only one log cabin. Because there were no docking sites, ships had to unload their cargo directly onto the beach, where people tried to move their goods before high tide. Inevitably, cargo was lost in the process. Some travelers had arrived intending to supply goods and services to the would-be miners; some of these miners, in turn, realizing how difficult reaching Dawson would be, chose to do the same. Within weeks, storehouses, saloons and offices lined the muddy streets of Dyea and Skagway, surrounded by tents and small, squalid shacks.

Skagway became famous in international media; the author John Muir described the town as "a nest of ants taken into a strange country and stirred up by a stick." While Dyea remained a transit point throughout the winter, Skagway began to take on a more permanent character. Skagway also built wharves out into the bay in order to attract a greater share of the prospectors. The town was effectively lawless, dominated by drinking, gunfire and prostitution. Visiting NWMP superintendent Samuel Benfield Steele, who arrived on June 24, 1898, and had no authority there, noted that Skagway was "little better than a hell on earth...about the roughest place in the world." Nonetheless, by the summer of 1898, with a population—including transients—of between fifteen thousand and twenty thousand, Skagway was the largest city in Alaska.

In late summer 1897, Skagway and Dyea fell under the control of Jefferson Randolph "Soapy" Smith and his men, who arrived from Seattle shortly after the Skagway population explosion. He was an American con man whose gang, said to be as large as two hundred to three hundred strong, cheated and stole from the prospectors traveling through the region. He maintained the illusion of being an upstanding member of the community, opening three saloons as well as creating fake businesses to assist in his operations. One of his scams was a fake telegraph office charging to send messages all over the United States and Canada, often pretending to receive a reply. Those replies would often mention a vague problem and urge the prospector to send money (which would never be delivered). Opposition to Smith steadily grew, and after weeks of vigilante activity, he was killed in Skagway during the shootout on Juneau Wharf in July 1898.

Other towns also boomed. Wrangell, a port of the Stikine route and a boomtown from earlier gold rushes, increased in size again, with robberies, gambling and nude female dancing becoming commonplace. Valdez, formed on the Gulf of Alaska during the attempt to create the All-American route, became a tent city of people who stayed behind to supply other ill-fated attempts to reach the interior. Edmonton in Alberta increased from a population of twelve hundred before the gold rush to four thousand during 1898. Beyond the immediate region, cities such as San Francisco, Seattle, Tacoma, Portland, Vancouver and Victoria all saw their populations soar as a result of the stampede and the trade the rush brought along. Between 1890 and 1900, Portland's population grew by an astonishing 95 percent (almost doubling). Vancouver grew even more—97 percent—while Seattle expanded by 88 percent. The rush would have the lasting impact of turning these modest cities—despite being nowhere near the actual site of gold claims—into major metropolitan areas.

Dawson City was created in the early days of the Klondike Gold Rush, when French Canadian prospector Joseph Francis Ladue (formerly of Deadwood) decided to make a profit from the influx of fortune seekers. He bought 178 acres of boggy mudflats at the junction of the Klondike and Yukon Rivers from the government and laid out the street plan for a new town, bringing in timber and other supplies to sell to the migrants. His sawmill was running night and day to build houses he could sell for $5,000 each, and he further supplemented his income by opening the first saloon. The town was named Dawson City after Ladue's friend George Mercer Dawson, the director of Canada's Geographical Survey. The city grew rapidly to hold five hundred people by the winter of 1896. In an all-too-familiar move, a Han village along Deer Creek was considered to be too close to the new town, and NWMP superintendent Charles Constantine (Steele's predecessor) moved its inhabitants three miles downriver to a small reserve.

In the spring of 1898, Dawson's population rose further to an impressive thirty thousand as stampeders arrived over the passes. The main thoroughfare, Front Street, was lined with hastily built buildings and warehouses, together with log cabins and tents spreading out across the rest of the settlement. There was no running water or drainage and only two springs for drinking water to supplement the increasingly polluted river. In spring, the unpaved streets were stomped and rolled into thick mud; in summer, the settlement reeked of fecal matter and other waste and was plagued by flies and mosquitoes. Land in Dawson had become scarce, and plots that had gone for $500 two years before sold for up to $10,000 each. Prime locations on Front Street could reach $20,000, while a small log cabin might rent for $100 a month. As a result, Dawson's population spread south into the empty Han village, renamed Klondike City. Other communities emerged closer to the mines, such as Granville on Dominion Creek and Grand Forks on Bonanza Creek.

The newly built town proved highly vulnerable to fire. Houses were made of wood, heated with stoves and lit by candles and oil lamps. Water for emergencies was lacking, especially in the frozen winters. The first major fire occurred on November 25, 1897, started accidentally by dance-hall girl Belle Mitchell.

Mitchell also accidentally started a second major fire on October 14, 1898. While staying at the Green Tree tavern, Mitchell had an argument with her friend Toni Page that escalated to the point where Mitchell threw a lantern in disgust. It quickly doused the room with oil and flame. In the absence of a fire brigade in Dawson, the blaze destroyed two major saloons, Alex

McDonald's post office building and the Bank of British North America at a cost of $500,000. Dawson's response to the 1898 fire was not helped by the refusal of the town to pay $12,000 for firefighting equipment that had been delivered but not released by the importers, who demanded payment. The equipment remained unused during the widespread inferno.

The worst incident occurred on April 26, 1899, when a saloon caught fire in the middle of a strike by the newly established fire brigade. Most of the major landmarks in the town burned to the ground. In all, 117 buildings were destroyed, with the damage estimated at over $1 million. Ironically, in late 1897, before the first fire, Dawson City flooded.

The remoteness of Dawson proved an ongoing problem for the supply of food, and as the population grew to five thousand in 1897, this became critical. When the rivers froze over, the realization that there would not be enough food for that winter became clear. The NWMP evacuated some prospectors without supplies to Fort Yukon in Alaska from September 30 onward, while others had already made their way out of the Klondike in search of food and shelter for the winter. The American government had five hundred reindeer sent from Norway across the United States and up the Dalton trail to Dawson as relief. However, they did not arrive until long after the risk of starvation was over. In the meantime, many of the animals themselves had died from hunger.

Prices remained high in Dawson, and supply fluctuated along with the seasons. During the winter of 1897, salt became worth its weight in gold, while nails, vital for construction work, rose in price to $28 per pound. Cans of butter sold for $5 each. The only eight horses in Dawson were slaughtered for dog food as they could not be kept alive over the winter. A good team of dogs was worth at least $1,000; a top set could reach $1,700. But in the desperate winter of 1897–98, the price reached $500 per dog. By the summer of 1898, approximately five thousand dogs had arrived at Dawson. A dog could pull as much as a man and much faster. Some were imported from outside the region; native dogs, however, were considered superior. They had been bred with wolves but were reportedly kind and easily handled. The first fresh goods arriving in the spring of 1898 sold for record prices, eggs reaching $3 each and apples $1.

Under these conditions, scurvy, a potentially fatal illness caused by the lack of vitamin C, proved a major problem in Dawson City, particularly during the winter, when supply of fresh food was not available. English prospectors gave scurvy the local name "Canadian black leg" on account of the unpleasant effects of the condition. Scurvy struck, among others, budding novelist Jack London. Although not fatal in his case, it brought an end to his mining career and made his front teeth fall out. As he later wrote, "I brought nothing back from the Klondike but my scurvy."

Dysentery and malaria were also common in Dawson, and an epidemic of typhoid broke out and ran rampant throughout the summer. Up to 140 patients were taken into the newly constructed St. Mary's Hospital, and thousands were affected. Measures were taken by the following year to prevent further outbreaks, including the introduction of better sewage management and the piping in of water from farther upstream, where fewer people had relieved themselves. These decisions provided some health improvements in 1899, although typhoid remained a problem. The new Han reserve, however, lay downstream from Dawson City, and here the badly contaminated river of urine and feces continued to contribute to epidemics of typhoid and diphtheria throughout the gold rush.

Despite these challenges, the huge quantities of gold coming through Dawson City encouraged a lavish lifestyle among the richer prospectors. Saloons were typically open twenty-four hours a day, with whiskey the standard drink. Gambling was popular, with the major saloons each running their own rooms. A culture of high stakes quickly became the norm, with rich prospectors routinely betting $1,000 at dice or playing for a $5,000 poker pot. The biggest recorded poker game in Dawson occurred between the well-known gamblers "Silent Sam" Bonnifeld and Louis "Goldie" Golden. Between $175,000 and $200,000 (sources vary) was put into the pot, which Bonnifeld won with a hand of four kings over Golden's four queens. Bonnifeld may have been a degenerate gambler, but he was honest, and no one doubted his luck.

The establishments around Front Street had grand façades in a Parisian style, mirrors and plate-glass windows and, from late 1898, were lit by electric light. The dance halls in Dawson were particularly prestigious and major status symbols, both for customers and their owners. Wealthy prospectors were expected to drink champagne at $60 a bottle, and the Pavilion dance hall cost its owner, Charlie Kimball, as much as $100,000 to construct and decorate. Elaborate opera houses were built, bringing singers and specialty acts to Dawson. Kimball is said to have made $12,000 on his dance hall's opening night and then spent the next three months on a $300,000 bender that ended in his financial and physical ruin.

Countless tales existed of prospectors spending huge sums on entertainment. Most payments were made in gold dust, and in places like saloons there was so much spilled gold that a profit could be made just by sweeping the floor. Some of the richest prospectors lived ostentatiously in Dawson. "Swiftwater" Bill Gates, a gambler and ladies' man who rarely went anywhere without wearing silk and diamonds, was one of them. To impress dance-hall girl Gussie Lamore, who liked eggs (an expensive luxury), he was alleged to have bought all the eggs in Dawson (said to be twenty-two hundred), had them boiled and fed them to wild dogs. A variation of the story said he bought the eggs and purposely let them rot. Another miner threw a sequence of gold objects onto the ship when his favorite singer left Dawson City as tokens of his esteem. The wealthiest dance-hall girls followed suit. Vaudevillian Daisy D'Avara had a belt made for herself from $340 in gold dollar coins; another, "Diamond Tooth" Gertie Lovejoy, alias Honora Ornstein, had a diamond inserted between her two front teeth. The miner and businessman Alex McDonald, despite being styled the "King of the Klondike," was unusual among his peers for his lack of grandiose spending.

Unlike its American equivalents, Dawson City was a law-abiding town. By 1897, 96 members of the NWMP had been sent to the district, and by 1898, this had increased to 288, an expensive commitment by the Canadian government. By June 1898, the force was headed by Colonel Sam Steele, an officer with a reputation for firm discipline. In 1898, there were no murders and only a few major thefts; in all, only about 150 arrests were made in the Yukon for serious offenses that year. Of these arrests, over half were for prostitution and resulted from an attempt by the NWMP to regulate the sex industry in Dawson. Regular monthly arrests, fifty-dollar fines and medical inspections were imposed, with the proceeds being used to fund the local hospitals.

The "blue laws" were strictly enforced. Saloons and other establishments closed promptly at midnight on Saturday, and anyone caught working on Sunday was likely to be fined or set to chopping firewood for the NWMP. The NWMP and Canadian government facilities needed enough wood each year to require a log pile two miles long by four feet wide. Up to fifty prisoners worked on cutting wood at any one time; this was not easy work and formed an unpleasant deterrent for misdemeanors. The NWMP was generally regarded to have been an efficient and honest force during the period, although its duties were helped by the geography of the Klondike, which made it relatively easy to bar entry to undesirables or prevent suspects from leaving the region.

In contrast to the NWMP, the early civil authorities were criticized by the prospectors for being incompetent and potentially corrupt. Thomas Fawcett was the gold commissioner and temporary head of the Klondike administration at the start of the gold rush; he was accused of keeping the details of new claims secret and allowing what one historian termed "carelessness, ignorance and partiality" to reign in the mine recorder's office. Or, in a word, he was sloppy. More generous accounts say he was merely in over his head. He entered the job with one hundred thousand papers to process and even slept in his office to prevent theft.

Following campaigns against Fawcett by prospectors, who were backed by the local press, Fawcett was relieved by the Canadian government. His successor, Major James Morrow Walsh, was a stronger character and arrived in May 1898 but fell ill and returned east in July. It was left to his replacement, William Ogilvie, supported by a Royal Commission, to conduct reforms. The commission, lacking any conclusive evidence, cleared Fawcett of all charges, which meant that he was not punished beyond his unjust termination. Ogilvie proved to be an administrator with an iron fist and subsequently revisited many of the mining surveys of his predecessors. As previously noted, he kept precise measurements.

In the remote Klondike, there was great demand for news and contact with the outside world. During the first months of the stampede in 1897, no news was too old to be read. In the lack of newspapers, some prospectors would read can labels until they knew them by heart. The following year, two teams fought their way over the passes to reach Dawson City first, complete with printing presses, with the aim of gaining control of the newspaper market. George M. Allen, the editor of the *Klondike Nugget*, arrived first but without his equipment, and it was the team behind the *Midnight Sun* who produced the first daily newspaper in Dawson. The *Dawson Miner* followed shortly after, bringing the number of daily newspapers in the town to three. The *Nugget* sold for twenty-four dollars as an annual subscription and became well known for championing miners and for its lucid coverage of scandals. Unused paper was often hard to find, and during the winter of 1898–99, the *Nugget* had to be printed on butcher's wrapping paper. In June 1898, a prospector bought an edition of the *Seattle Post-Intelligencer* at an auction and charged spectators one dollar each to have the paper read aloud in one of Dawson's halls.

Mail service was chaotic during the stampede. Apart from the sheer number of prospectors, two major obstacles stood in its way. To begin with, any mail from America to Dawson City was sent to Juneau in southeast Alaska before being sent through Dawson and then down the Yukon to Circle City. From here, the mail was then distributed by the U.S. Post Office back up to Dawson. The huge distances involved resulted in delays of several months and frequently the loss of protective envelopes and their addresses. The second problem was in Dawson itself, which initially lacked a post office and therefore relied on two stores and a saloon to act as informal delivery points. The NWMP was tasked to run the mail system, but it was not properly prepared to do so. Up to fifty-seven hundred letters might arrive in a single shipment, all of which had to be collected in person from the post office. This resulted in long waits, with claimants lining up outside the office for up to three days. Those who had no time and could afford it would pay others to stand in line for them, preferably a woman, since they were allowed to get ahead in line out of politeness. Postage stamps, like paper in general, were scarce and rationed to two per customer. By 1899, trained postal staff took over mail delivery and relieved the NWMP of this task.

In 1898, 8 percent of those living in the Klondike territory were women, and in more established towns like Dawson, this rose to 12 percent. Many women arrived with their husbands or families, but a few brave others traveled alone. Most came to the Klondike for similar economic and social reasons as had male prospectors, but they attracted particular media interest. The gender imbalance in the Klondike encouraged business proposals to ship young, single women into the region to marry newly wealthy miners. Few, if any, of these marriages ever took place, but some single women appear to have traveled on their own in the hope of finding prosperous husbands.

Guidebooks gave recommendations for what practical clothes women should take to the Klondike. The female dress code of the time was formal, emphasizing long skirts and corsets, but most women adapted this for the conditions of the trails. Regardless of experience, women in a party were typically expected to cook for the group. Few mothers brought their children with them, due to the risks of travel and the remote location.

Once in the Klondike, very few women—less than 1 percent—actually worked as miners. Many were married to miners; however, their lives as partners on the gold fields were still hard and often lonely. They had extensive domestic duties, including thawing ice and snow for water, breaking up frozen food, chopping wood and collecting wild foods. In Dawson and other towns, some women took in laundry to make money. This was a physically demanding job but could be relatively easily combined with childcare duties. Others took jobs in the service industry, for example as waitresses or seamstresses. These could pay well but were often broken up by periods of unemployment. Both men and women opened roadhouses, but women were considered to be better at running them. A few women worked in the packing trade, carrying goods on their backs, or became domestic servants.

Wealthier women with disposable income might invest in mines and other businesses. One of the most prominent entrepreneurs in the Klondike was Irish immigrant Belinda Mulrooney, purportedly the "richest woman in the Klondike." She brought a consignment of cloth and hot-water bottles with her when she arrived in the Klondike in early 1897. With the proceeds of those sales (said to be a 600 percent profit) she first built a roadhouse at Grand Forks and later the elegrant Fair View Hotel in Dawson. She invested widely, including acquiring her own mining company. The wealthy Martha Munger-Black was abandoned by her husband early in the journey to the Klondike (he fled to Hawaii) but continued on without him, reaching Dawson City, where she became a prominent citizen, investing in various mining and business ventures with her brother.

A relatively small number of women worked in the entertainment and sex industries. The elite of these women were the highly paid actresses and courtesans of Dawson; below them were chorus-line dancers, who usually doubled as hostesses and other dance-hall workers. While still better paid than white-collar male workers, these women worked very long hours and had significant expenses. The entertainment industry overlapped with the sex industry, where women made a living as prostitutes. The sex industry in the Klondike was concentrated in Klondike City and in a red-light district of Dawson. A hierarchy of sexual employment existed, with brothels and parlor houses at the top, small independent "cigar shops" in the middle and, at the bottom, prostitutes who worked out of small huts called "hutches." Life for these workers was a continual struggle, and the suicide rate was high.

The degree of involvement between native women and the stampeders varied. Many Tlingit women worked as packers for the prospectors, for example, carrying supplies and equipment, sometimes even transporting their babies. Han women had relatively little contact with the white immigrants, however, and there was a significant social divide between local Han women and white women. Although before 1897 there had been a number of native women who married western men, including Kate Carmack (real name Shaaw Tláa), this practice did not survive into the stampede. Very few stampeders married Han women. "Respectable" white women would avoid associating with native women or prostitutes; those who did could cause scandal.

By 1899, telegraphy stretched from Skagway to Dawson City, allowing instant international contact. In 1898, the White Pass and Yukon Route railway began to be built between Skagway and the head of navigation on the Yukon. When the railway was completed in 1900, the Chilkoot trail and its tramways were obsolete. Despite these improvements in communication and transport, the rush faltered from 1898 on. The decline began in summer 1898, when many of the prospectors arriving in Dawson City found themselves unable to make a living and left for home. For those who stayed, the wages of casual work fell to $100 a month by 1899. The world's newspapers began to turn against the Klondike Gold Rush as well. In April 1898, the Spanish-American War removed the gold rush from the headlines. "Ah, go to the Klondike!" became a popular phrase of disgust. The recently trendy Klondike-branded goods had to be disposed of at special rates in Seattle. Dan Seavey was coming in just as others were going out.

Another factor in the decline was the change in Dawson City, which had developed throughout 1898, transforming from a largely inadequate, if wealthy, boomtown into a peaceful, conservative municipality. Modern luxuries were introduced, including the "zinc bath tubs and pianos, billiard tables, Brussels carpets in the hotel dining rooms, menus printed in French and invitational balls" noted by later histories. The visiting California politician Jeremiah Lynch likened the newly paved streets with their smartly dressed inhabitants to the Strand in London. Dawson City was no longer as attractive a location for many prospectors, used to a wilder way of living. Even the formerly lawless town of Skagway had become a stable and respectable community by 1899.

The final trigger, however, was the discovery of gold elsewhere in Canada and Alaska, prompting a new stampede, this time away from the Klondike. In August 1898, gold had been found at Atlin Lake at the head of the Yukon River, generating a buzz of interest, but in September 1898, much larger quantities were found at Nome at the mouth of the Yukon. In 1899, a flood of prospectors from across the region left for Nome, eight thousand from Dawson alone during a single week in August. The Klondike Gold Rush was over.

Only a handful of the one hundred thousand people who left for the Klondike during the gold rush became rich. They typically spent $1,000 each reaching the region, which, when combined, exceeded what was produced from the gold fields between 1897 and 1901. At the same time, most of those who did find gold lost their fortunes in the subsequent years. They often died penniless, attempting to reproduce their earlier good fortune in fresh mining opportunities. Businessman and miner Alex McDonald, for example, continued to accumulate land after the boom until his money ran out; he died in poverty, still prospecting. George Carmack left his wife,

Kate—who had found it difficult to adapt to their new lifestyle—remarried and lived in relative prosperity. Skookum Jim had a huge income from his mining royalties but refused to settle and continued to prospect until his death in 1916. Dawson Charlie spent lavishly and died in an alcohol-related accident. Kate died during the Spanish flu pandemic of 1918.

The richest of the Klondike saloon owners, businessmen and gamblers also typically lost their fortunes and died in poverty. George M. Allen, the editor of the *Klondike Nugget*, became bankrupt and spent the rest of his career in smaller newspapers. The prominent gambler and saloon owner Sam Bonnifield suffered a nervous breakdown, spent time in an insane asylum and died in extreme poverty after being hit by a car. Nonetheless, some of those who joined the gold rush prospered. Kathleen "Klondike Kate" Rockwell, for example, became a famous dancer and brothel keeper in Dawson and remained popular in America until her death. Dawson City was also where Alexander Pantages, her Greek business partner and boyfriend, started his vaudeville career, going on to become one of America's greatest movie theater tycoons before his fall from grace following sexual assault allegations. The sawmill owner Martha Munger-Black remarried and ultimately became the second female member of the Canadian parliament.

The gold rush had a considerable impact on the native peoples of the region. The Tlingit and the Koyukon peoples prospered in the short term from their work as guides and packers and from selling food and supplies to the prospectors. In the longer term, however, the Han people living in the Klondike region suffered from the environmental damage of gold mining on the rivers and forests. Their population had already begun to decline after the discovery of gold along Fortymile River in the 1880s but dropped catastrophically after their move to the reserve, a result of the contaminated water supply and smallpox. The Han found only a few ways to benefit economically from the gold rush, and their fishing and hunting grounds were largely destroyed. By 1904, they needed aid from the NWMP to prevent famine.

Dawson City declined after the gold rush. When journalist Laura Beatrice Berton moved to Dawson in 1907, the boomtown was still thriving, but away from Front Street the town had become increasingly deserted and jammed "with the refuse of the gold rush: stoves, furniture, gold-pans, sets of dishes, double-belled seltzer bottles…piles of rusting mining machinery—boilers, winches, wheelbarrows and pumps." By 1912, only around two thousand inhabitants remained, compared to the thirty thousand of the boom years. The site was becoming a ghost town. By 1972, five hundred people were living in Dawson, whereas the nearby settlements created during the gold rush had been entirely abandoned. The population has grown since the 1970s, with a modest thirteen hundred recorded in 2006.

During the gold rush, transport improvements meant that heavier mining equipment could be brought in and larger, more modern mines established in the Klondike, revolutionizing the gold industry. As a result of the dredging and hydraulic mining, gold production increased each year until 1903 but then declined. By 2005, approximately 1,250,000 pounds had been recovered from the Klondike area. In the twenty-first century, Dawson City still has a small gold-mining industry, which together with tourism plays a role in the local economy. Many buildings in the center of town still reflect the style of the era.

The port of Skagway also shrank after the rush, but it remains a well-preserved period town, centered on the tourist industry and sightseeing trips from visiting cruise ships. Restoration work by the National Park Service began in 2010 on Jeff Smith's Parlor, from which "Soapy" Smith once operated. Skagway also has one of the two visitor centers forming the Klondike Gold Rush National Historical Park. The other is located in Seattle, and both focus on the human-interest stories behind the gold rush. The railway built for prospectors through White Pass in the last year of the rush reopened in 1988 and is today used only by tourists. It is closely linked to the Chilkoot trail, which is a popular hiking route.

The events of the Klondike Gold Rush rapidly became embedded in North American culture, being captured in poems, stories, photographs and promotional campaigns long after the end of the stampede. In the Yukon, Discovery Day is celebrated on the third Monday in August as a holiday, and the events of the gold rush are promoted by the regional tourist industries. The events of the gold rush were frequently exaggerated at the time, and modern works on the subject similarly often focus on the most dramatic and exciting events of the stampede, not always accurately. Yukon-raised historian Ken Coates describes the gold rush as "a resilient, pliable myth" that continues to fascinate and appeal.

Several novels, books and poems were generated as a consequence of the Klondike Gold Rush. The writer Jack London incorporated scenes from the gold rush into his novels and short stories set in the Klondike, including *The Call of the Wild* (1903), a novel about a sled dog named Buck who grows increasingly primitive when subjected to the wilderness. London's colleague, poet Robert W. Service (1874–1958), did not join the rush himself, although he made his home in Dawson City in 1908. Service created well-known poems about the gold rush, among them those in *Songs of a Sourdough* (1907), one of the bestselling poetry collections in the early twentieth century, along with his novel *The Trail of Ninety-Eight* (1909), written by hand on wallpaper in one of Dawson's log cabins.

Some terminology from the stampede made its way into American English, including *cheechakos*, translated as "newcomers" and referring to newly arrived miners, and *sourdoughs*, experienced miners. Jack London famously captured the origins of these terms, describing how "the men who came ashore from the steamers were newcomers. They were known as *chechaquos*, and they always wilted at the application of the name. They made their bread with baking-powder. This was the invidious distinction between them and the Sour-doughs, who, forsooth, made their bread from sour-dough because they had no baking-powder."

The photographs taken during the Klondike Gold Rush heavily influenced later cultural approaches to the stampede. The gold rush was vividly recorded by photographer Eric A. Hegg; his stark, black-and-white photographs showing the ascent of the Chilkoot Pass rapidly became iconic images and were widely distributed. These pictures in turn inspired Charlie Chaplin to make the classic film *The Gold Rush* (1925), which uses the background of the Klondike to combine physical comedy with its character's desperate battle for survival in the harsh conditions of the stampede. The photographs reappear in the documentary *City of Gold* (1957). Narrated by Pierre Berton, it won prizes for pioneering the incorporation of still images into documentary filmmaking. The Klondike Gold Rush, however, has not been widely covered in later fictional films; even *The Far Country* (1955), a Western set in the Klondike, largely ignores the unique features of the gold rush in favor of a traditional Western plot. Indeed, much of the popular literature on the gold rush approaches the stampede simply as a final phase of the expansion of the American West, a perception critiqued by modern historians such as the Yukon-born Charlene Porsild.

With all due respect to Porsild, while I appreciate how seeing the Yukon as part of Manifest Destiny is problematic, this view serves perfectly as a way to sum up the wanderlust of Dan Seavey and his family. From the first Seavey settling in New England, to Dan moving west to the rapidly expanding northwoods and then again to the boomtowns of Alaska…what better way to describe this multigenerational sense of adventure?

More specifically with the Yukon, where does Seavey and the Rosebud Mining Company fit into all of this? Did he make his fortune or walk away destitute? For the most part, we do not know his exploits. What route did he take? In which city did he stay? If this could have been determined, we would be able to narrow down coverage of the gold rush—but any of these problems or colorful characters could have been part of the Seavey story. We really know very little. As Seavey later recalled, five test beds were made, and then the funds began to dry up. "The only time I made any real money in Alaska," he said, "was when I got $500 for hoisting up a large safe that had fallen through the floor of a saloon. There was a lot of money in the safe, and the owners had been trying for a couple of weeks to raise her up to the main floor. One of them came up to me and asked how much I would do the job for. He had overheard me make some remarks about how they were bungling the job, I guess. I said that if he would give me eight men and $500 I would do it. He accepted the offer, and I went and got some ropes and poles. In a half hour, I had the safe out of the cellar." The test beds came up empty, Rosebud was unsuccessful and Seavey returned to the Great Lakes region one year later completely broke.

In one version of the story, Mary Seavey and their two daughters did not even know where Dan had gone after the failure in Alaska, and spent time looking for him, for a while visiting Dan's father and stepmother, who were as confused as Mary was. A tip came one day that Dan was tending bar in a saloon. Mary did, indeed, find him there, but he had no desire to return to his family.

Regardless of how their split happened, after Dan deserted her, Mary Seavey returned to northern Wisconsin. She married William J. Steele, moved to Sagola, upper Michigan (near Iron Mountain) around 1900 and raised a family of seven additional children: Darius, William, Delphine, Melvina, Harold, Rosie and Amanda (known as Goldie). Steele worked variously as a day laborer and a jobber for the local lumber company. So far as can be gleaned from the records, Mary never formally requested or received a divorce from Dan.

As far as the gold rush is concerned, the entire adventure was such a bust that Dan Seavey was already back in the upper Lake Michigan area by late 1899, now employed in the career that made him infamous. The timeline suggests he spent a year at most in Alaska, but more likely only half that. The *Sturgeon Bay Advocate* reported him working for John E. Stephan (1868–1936), hauling eighty tons of hay from Baileys Harbor, Wisconsin, to Frankfort, Michigan, between November 7 and 22. His ship, the *Rambler*, described as a "scow schooner," had only one member of the crew: his sister Jennie, who served as his cook. Distinct from other schooners, scow schooners had a broad, shallow hull and used centerboards, bilgeboards or leeboards rather than a deep keel. The broad hull gave them stability, and the retractable foils allowed them to move even heavy loads of cargo in waters far too shallow for keelboats to enter. The squared-off bow and stern accommodated a large cargo. Such designs evolved around the time of the American colonies and faded away in the early 1900s.

3

AFTER ALASKA

ESCANABA

As of August 1900, Seavey still sailed the *Rambler* and worked for Stephan; he was reported to bring in a shipload of 280,000 shingles from Baileys Harbor to the Lyon dock in Sturgeon Bay. After dropping off the shingles, Seavey set sail for Pentwater, Michigan, to gather a load of fruit. When the census taker came around that year, Seavey lived at Crystal Lake township, Benzie County, Michigan, with sister Jennie. The rest of his family does not appear to have lived with them. Crystal Lake is a "suburb" of Frankfort, though that term is a stretch in a county that had perhaps ten thousand people at most.

Seavey sold the *Rambler* to Messenger and Paige of Jacksonport in September 1900. Days later, the ship was sold again to Captain John Devine of Sturgeon Bay for $320, and Devine immediately set out for Sheboygan with a load of cordwood.

Devine was well known in his day, perhaps almost as much as Seavey himself. He had been born in Limerick, Ireland, in 1844 and immigrated to the United States with his parents as a child, settling in Kewaunee County not long after Wisconsin's statehood. John became a patriarch of a notable sailing family, with three sons following their father to the sea: Henry was an engineer on the government tug *Manitowoc*; John II sailed on a Hines barge; and William was seeking his fortune at sea as well. Captain John Devine passed away in October 1914 from "a general breakdown and complication of diseases" at age seventy-one. His final home was the Hotel Malvetz in Sturgeon Bay.

By late 1900, Seavey had moved to Escanaba, Michigan, and acquired a forty-foot schooner, which he named the *Wanderer*, a suitable successor name to the *Rambler*. With this ship, Seavey began moonlighting as a pirate to supplement his legitimate income. As the story goes, the *Wanderer* had originally cost $6,000 when built by the Pabst family and was said to be "the handsomest pleasure yacht." Once Seavey took possession, he seems to have gutted the ship but kept the luxurious cabin and captain's quarters. Though the Pabst family is most often associated with brewing, they were also avid sailors and made the occasional investment in other ventures, such as gold mining, as we have seen. Yet, is the Pabst story even true? Records for the ship neglect to mention Pabst at all but point to the original owner as a J.F. Sanderson.

Escanaba was the name of an Ojibwe village in the early nineteenth century. The Ojibwe are one of the Algonquian-speaking tribes who settled and flourished around the Great Lakes. The word *Escanaba* roughly translates from Ojibwe and other regional Algonquian languages to "land of the red buck," although some people maintain that the name refers to "flat rock," as in the smooth, flat rocks found in the Escanaba River (hence its name). The closest language to Ojibwe is Ottawa, though both Menominee and Potawatomi are similar, and these various tribes have many overlapping words. (Think of Spanish and Italian; though different, their Latin roots are close enough that it is quite possible to understand one if you know the other.)

As a European American settlement, the Escanaba we know today was founded in 1863 as a port town by surveyor Eli Parsons Royce (1820–1912), who worked for lumber tycoon Nelson Ludington. The town's first major industry was the processing and harvesting of lumber, dominated in this area by Ludington, Daniel Wells and Jefferson Sinclair. Nelson Ludington & Company had been in the lumber business since 1848 and recognized that the rapid expansion of western towns around the Great Lakes would increase market demand for lumber. Ludington bought up large tracts of timberlands in the Upper Peninsula; he also constructed various mills to process the lumber.

Ludington later moved his headquarters to Chicago, where he expanded his business portfolio into banking. Isaac Stephenson established a successor lumber company in the Escanaba area and also became a "capitalist," or what we would today more commonly call an investor.

Before the Civil War, iron ore was being mined from the Marquette Range and shipped out on barges from Escanaba. The port was also important

A ship at the ore dock in Escanaba in 1898. *Library of Congress.*

to the Union as a shipping point for these ores, in addition to lumber. Soon after it became a town in 1863, Escanaba was quickly growing as an important shipping port. The Peninsula Railroad was completed in 1864, linking Escanaba to the iron mines of the Upper Peninsula to the north. Iron ore docks were built in the Escanaba harbor, and the shipping of iron ore to steel mills along the Great Lakes became Escanaba's leading industry.

The Menominee Range and Gogebic Range of upper Michigan became important for iron ore a bit later than Marquette, in the 1880s. In fact, Michigan still produces about 25 percent of the iron ore nationally. Initially, lumber was still integral to shipbuilding, and supported the construction of houses in cities throughout the developing Midwest. Iron ore supported industrialization and became part of steel and other industries in the Midwest.

As shipping increased, a lighthouse was needed to warn of sand shoals in Little Bay de Noc, which extended from Escanaba's Sand Point, a thin, sandy peninsula located just south of and adjacent to the harbor area. The United States Lighthouse Service approved construction of the Sand Point

Lighthouse at a cost of $11,000. Construction began in the fall of 1867 and was completed in early spring 1868. The light first shone on the night of May 13, 1868.

The Sand Point Lighthouse is a story-and-a-half rectangular building with an attached brick tower. The tower is topped with a cast-iron lantern room that houses a fourth-order Fresnel lens, emitting a fixed red light with a radiating power of eleven and a half miles. A unique distinction concerning the Sand Point Lighthouse is that the building was constructed with its tower facing the land instead of facing the water. Whether this orientation was intentional or an engineering blunder is unknown. The building still stands today as part of the Delta County Historical Society.

John Terry was appointed the first lighthouse keeper of the new lookout in December 1867, but he became very ill and died in April 1868, a month before the lighthouse was ready to be manned. With the lighthouse nearly completed but with no lightkeeper ready to report for duty, John Terry's widow, Mary, was appointed lightkeeper and subsequently became one of the first female lightkeepers on the Great Lakes. Mary, a well-respected citizen in the community, fulfilled her duties as lightkeeper with efficiency and dedication. She was lightkeeper from 1868 to 1886, when a mysterious fire severely damaged the lighthouse and took her life. To this day, no one knows exactly what happened or why it happened. Some speculate that the source of the fire was an attempted burglary and that the suspect set the lighthouse afire to cover any evidence of wrongdoing. The south entrance door showed signs of forced entry, yet none of Mary Terry's valuables were

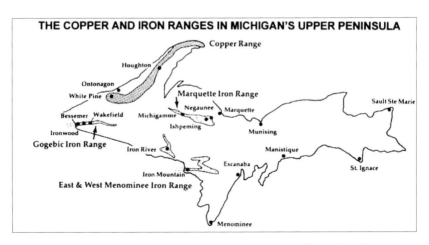

A diagram showing where the iron ore is in upper Michigan. *U.S. Geological Survey.*

The Sand Point Lighthouse in Escanaba. *Author's photo.*

taken. With the lighthouse badly damaged, restoration took nearly two full months. A new lightkeeper, Lewis Rose, was appointed to take over.

Author Walter Nursey compares Escanaba in this era to Bilbao, Spain, another major iron producer. He notes that in 1889, Bilbao had a population of fifty thousand inhabitants and was shipping out 3 million tons of iron ore that year. Escanaba had a population of only six thousand but managed to ship out 3.8 million tons. This small village was truly the "Iron Port of the World," and anyone set up for shipping (as Seavey was) could expect plenty of opportunities. Nursey also speaks of the high quality of lumber and laments that the wood had to be sent by rail to Kaukauna (southwest of Green Bay) for use in the pulp mills. He suggests that had the locals developed a pulp process, the lumber industry would have been even more profitable. Indeed, had Escanaba rather than northeast Wisconsin become a paper mill epicenter, it would be interesting to see how this would shift the population over time.

This book's author, a native of northeast Wisconsin, can speak from personal experience that the stretch of cities from Green Bay to Oshkosh owes its existence to the paper industry. Dozens of mills dotted the Fox

River, creating millionaires who funded city parks, schools and museums. Thousands of workers, often multiple generations of the same families, worked in the mills and were able to provide comfortable middle-class lives for their children. How the region would have grown differently from the 1870s and beyond without paper is an impossible "what if" to imagine.

Isaac Stephenson, the logging magnate, expanded his empire in 1897 when he built a modest, seven-mile railway to haul his logs. This company, the Escanaba & Lake Superior Railway (later Railroad), continued to thrive, and today it operates hundreds of miles of track while other companies have failed or been bought out. The lines still primarily service Michigan's Upper Peninsula, with routes heading south to Green Bay and west to Ontonagon on the Lake Superior shore.

To be sure, at the time Seavey arrived in Escanaba, the town was a thriving industrial community and the ideal home of an enterprising entrepreneur, adventurer and individualist. The world was his oyster.

His first order of business was to find another bride. Seavey married Exilda "Zilda" Bisner on January 30, 1901, in Escanaba in front of Emil Glaser (1841–1923), justice of the peace. She was the daughter of Joseph Bisner and Mary Walker. On the certificate, Seavey gave his occupation as "marine-man." Witnesses were Jennie A. Glaser (Emil's wife) and Mrs. Sarah J. Dix (Jennie's mother), both of Escanaba. Having the justice's wife and elderly mother-in-law as witnesses suggests that the new couple had few friends. On the document, Seavey swore he had "no previous marriages"—a lie. In fact, it is not even clear if Seavey had formally divorced his first wife. A brief item in the newspaper said that Zilda had only arrived from lower Michigan a few months prior. It also identified Seavey's schooner as "The Hustler," which is likely an error. Some questions must be asked: Did Zilda know that Dan had another wife? How did the two meet and marry so quickly?

Seavey and the *Wanderer* were delivering peaches in August 1901, first to Sturgeon Bay and then to Escanaba.

A year after Dan and Zilda's marriage, on May 7, 1902, Earl Daniel Seavey was born in Milwaukee. Earl would be Dan's only son, though his time on earth was short. His birth in Milwaukee is most strange, given that the Seavey family lived nowhere near that area and had no family in the city to my knowledge. John Mitchell would later claim that the *Wanderer* operated as "a floating gambling hall in Milwaukee harbor," though this was only hearsay and not experience. Nor is it likely that Dan would bring his pregnant wife with him on such ventures, if we wanted to explain why they were near Milwaukee in May 1902. According to Mitchell, the *Wanderer* was also "dealing in booze, stolen sawmills [*sic*] and other loot, bristling with pistols and shotguns and shanghaied girls, both red and white, whose easy virtues were traded for coin of the realm at all lake ports."

Within months of Earl's birth, and less than two years since the wedding, Zilda Seavey filed for divorce on August 26, 1902. In October, the divorce of Seavey and Zilda was "taken under advisement" in Kewaunee County Circuit Court. The matter went to trial in May 1903, with Zilda retaining John Wattawa (a one-time candidate for lieutenant governor) as her attorney. She sought custody of their son and ongoing child support and maintenance, as she had no occupation or property of her own. Zilda swore that Seavey "gives out and threatens that he will do violence" and that "unless restrained by the order of this court, he will carry out such threats." She further swore that Seavey planned to sell his ship, the *Wanderer*, and move across state lines in order to avoid paying alimony. She believed the ship to be valued at $800, on top of $1,000 cash Seavey had on him and holdings of real estate in Maine that she had never seen and did not know the value of.

Otto H. Bruemmer—a mayor, district attorney and bank president—represented Seavey in court and filed a response to Zilda's affidavit. Seavey acknowledged that Zilda was his wife, saying they had been married in Escanaba on January 20, 1891. This was false; the correct date was January 30, 1901. He conceded that Earl was his son and that he owned a vessel named the *Wanderer*. He denied every other charge: that he was violent, that he intended to sell his ship and that he would flee. Whether that last point was true is doubtful, as Seavey never personally appeared in court, being busy "sailing upon the Great Lakes." By May 15, the case was ordered dismissed.

Around November 1903, seven boys were arrested at Escanaba: George A. Boddy, John Horrigan, John Cleary, Connie O'Donnell, Raleigh Ralph Baum, George Lang and Nels Dishnaw. They had stolen "various articles" (not otherwise identified) from the Fair Savings Bank dry goods store run by Herman Salinsky. Boddy was given sixty days in jail, Horrigan had jumped bail and the other boys were sentenced to the state industrial school at Lansing by Justice Glaser. Some of the goods were recovered from Seavey's ship. He swore to authorities that he did not know he had purchased stolen goods from the boys, and he was not charged. How much he truly knew is speculation, but would the police have given Dan the benefit of the doubt if they knew who he would become?

Seavey allegedly fought noted pugilist Mitch Love in the winter of 1903–4 at Frankfort, Michigan. The fight was held on the ice of the frozen harbor, where a shoveled circle served as a makeshift ring. About two hundred people reportedly witnessed the contest, many placing sizable bets on the outcome. The contestants went at it eagerly with bare knuckles for some time between two and two and a half hours, depending on how exaggerated the story is on retelling. Radio broadcaster William Duchaine prefers the longer fight. Seavey eventually made a bloody pulp of Love, who was carted off for medical attention by his dejected supporters. Roaring Dan apparently cleaned up on the contest, not only collecting the main purse but also a percentage on numerous side bets placed by his cohorts. Confirmation of this tale is hard to come by, as no record of Mitch Love's very existence has been found in Frankfort or elsewhere.

A similar tale related Dan fighting an unnamed "he-man" in a Manistee tavern, with the pair breaking windows, doors and everything else before the law arrived. In Duchaine's words, "Dan heard of a rough and ready fighter in Manistee, and went there to find him. Meeting in a saloon, they had a few drinks together, then threw the crowd out and went to it. The place was a shambles when the law appeared and stopped the brawl just as Dan was finishing off his rival."

Author Thomas Edward Jacques tells a secondhand anecdote of Seavey's brawling worth quoting at length. He writes:

> *The author's grandmother used to tell him stories about old Dan Seavey coming to town to visit his favorite drinking establishments. One time she told how old Seavey had started a brawl in one of the local saloons in the Village of Garden and was finally chased through the streets by a large crowd of people. He escaped along the shore back of the now Marygrove property to Van's Harbor where his ship was at anchor out in the bay. He had been warned never to return again.*

Van's Harbor, today overgrown by trees and other plant life, had briefly been a small boomtown. The first known settler was allegedly Father DuCroix, a French missionary. Later reports described him as "rather eccentric," and no nearby residents "found it pleasant to visit his haunts after dark." Not surprisingly, his attempts to found a mission in the harbor failed. The titular Van was Lewis Van Winkle, who established a sawmill there in 1881. The mill was successful enough to support "five or six camps" along the Fish Dam River, and the men would bring in logs they floated from Big Bay de Noc. The logs would be transformed into sweet-smelling pine planks and loaded up on to schooners and "puffing side-wheelers" to be transported south along the lake. For twenty years nonstop, white pine and Norway pine made its way through the saw—no other wood was welcome. Van Winkle was known as the "lumber king of the garden Peninsula."

A large sawmill inevitably creates a great deal of wood waste, and a "burner" was constructed. Shaped roughly like a silo, and reaching eighty feet in height, this "voracious monster" (as the press called it) burned night and day, the surrounding woods protected by a lining of firebrick and a screen on top that allowed smoke to escape while keeping stray cinders in. At its peak, the mill supported a small hamlet of forty or fifty families, all owing their livelihood to Van Winkle. A railroad would not appear until much later, and at the time that Seavey made Van's Harbor one of his hangouts, "all land travel was affected by horse-drawn vehicles over tortuous sand roads that sometimes discouraged even the most hardy of travelers." We can presume a sailor would not find himself heading inland very far.

The *Wanderer* brought peaches from Arcadia, Michigan, to Sturgeon Bay from September through October 1904. October 3 and 4 brought in a strong southeast gale, with the *Wanderer* caught in the middle of the lake when the storm hit. Seavey was again hauling peaches from Arcadia, and his ship survived the voyage, but he lost his yawl when the water came over the sides of the boat, washing the yawl from the davits. The yawl was sixteen feet long, square at both ends and painted the color of lead. Based on the wind, Seavey estimated it would reach shore near Baileys Harbor. He further reported a large, two-masted schooner in distress on the morning of October 4. Seavey could not make out the name of the ship, but its flying jib and raffe were in shreds, and part of its load appeared to be missing.

If you, the reader, are like most nonsailors, the nautical terms in the preceding paragraph are not words you use on a regular basis. Apparently, readers of the Sturgeon Bay newspapers spoke sailor, but for those who don't: the yawl is a ship's small or medium boat stored onboard, used for general-purpose work, sometimes called a jolly boat. Think of the yawl as being like a dinghy or a lifeboat. A davit is a crane that projects over the side of a ship or a hatchway and is used for boats, anchors or cargo. In this case, the davits would be the two bars that lower the yawl into the water off the side of the ship. A jib is the triangular staysail set forward of the forwardmost mast, and the flying jib is the outermost jib. A raffe is the triangular topsail set above a square lower sail. So, in short, the storm disconnected Seavey's smaller boat from the side of his ship, and the other vessel he saw had its sails in tatters.

Seavey was spending a fair amount of time transporting hunting and fishing parties around November 5, 1904. He had recently carried loads of grapes, apples, potatoes and onions. The newspaper gave his home as Ludington, across the lake from Manitowoc and farther south than his usual hangouts.

Zilda filed for divorce again on March 17, 1905, this time in Escanaba, pleading her case as the victim of domestic abuse, and Seavey fled once again onto the lake. Richard Boyd says the document "describes several drunken tirades" and "scary death threats." He does not quote directly from the divorce record.

Earl Seavey was in the Escanaba hospital on October 31, 1905, according to a notation in the hospital records. What led to this visit is unknown, but it would prove to be ominous.

The wood steamer *John M. Nicol*, owned by the Nicol Transit Company of Buffalo, ran aground near Big Summer Island in the Green Bay on December 13, 1906. No lives were lost, and the twenty-one-man crew was rescued by two fishermen in a small gasoline launch who brought them to Escanaba. The sailors "suffered terribly from exposure and several of them have badly frozen hands and feet." They brought nothing with them but the clothes on their backs. Though the rumors could not be confirmed, it was suspected that Seavey soon after stole the ship's cargo. He was said to have a large quantity of gloves, shoes and leather for sale. The ship, however, was reported to have a cargo of $60,000 worth of barbed wire—not gloves or shoes. On another occasion, according to Jacques, he mysteriously had a "boatload of caviar" from an unknown source. The *Nicol* had been in decline for years, and its inevitable crash was likely no surprise to anyone. In 1890, it was valued at a staggering $135,000; this value decreased rapidly and was down to only $35,000 in 1904. That was still a sizable amount in those days, but the ship's best years were clearly in the past.

We know for sure that Seavey was not above scavenging from abandoned ships. The Edward Carus Collection, available at the Wisconsin Maritime Museum in Manitowoc, has a series of photographs showing Seavey and crew taking what they can from the steamer *Vega*. The *Vega* was stranded and partially sunk off South Fox Island, northeast Lake Michigan, in November 1905. Seavey showed up years later in this case, not in the cover of night, as alleged with the *John M. Nicol*.

Seavey sailed the *Wanderer* as a legitimate shipping operation but also sailed into ports at night to steal cargo from other vessels and warehouses. Seavey also allegedly kidnapped or transported women in the illegal prostitution

The *John M. Nicol*, in the days before Dan Seavey came along. *Wisconsin Maritime Museum.*

trade, called "painted ladies" in the press. This was an early form of human trafficking and sex trafficking. There is great doubt that any kidnapping occurred, but Seavey was no stranger to prostitution.

Seavey was notorious for altering sea lights, either by extinguishing existing lights or placing false lights. The trick, known as "moon cussing" or "cursing," would cause ships to sail into rocks, where Seavey's crew could easily capture the cargo from the wounded vessel. He was never caught in the act, but rumors persisted.

A significant amount of Seavey's profit was made from venison poaching at Summer Island and St. Martin Island, both off the Garden Peninsula. When a company called Booth Fisheries, or more properly the A. Booth Fish Company of Chicago, attempted to compete with Seavey's illegal venison trade, Seavey allegedly attacked one of its ships with a cannon, killing everyone on board. Finding any record of this event, or even of Seavey possessing a cannon, has so far eluded me, and no doubt this is yet another exaggerated or completely fabricated tale that has been passed on enough times that the story is taken as fact. Where he would acquire a cannon is not known, and the possibility of his "killing everyone on board" is nonexistent. Even if Seavey were capable of murder (something we have no evidence of), there is no way the authorities would simply turn a blind eye.

Zilda Seavey was in the hospital on February 28, 1907. Why she was there may never be known, but Dan was with her and paid in cash for her stay. Their turbulent time together was not quite over.

In general, 1907 was an incredibly good year for the sailors of Lake Michigan, especially the massive freighters. Shipping costs by freighter were so much more affordable than train, leading to customers saving an estimated $173 million that year on the transport of iron ore compared to what it would have cost by rail. Along with ore, timber and wheat were also moving across the lake from Michigan and Wisconsin. The upper Midwest had been a frontrunner in wheat production for decades, making Lakes Michigan and Superior ideal places to export the grain to the rest of the country.

Seavey was not a freighter captain, but he surely would have benefited from the economy indirectly. The iron ore coming out of upper Michigan had created boomtowns throughout the wilderness. Although closer to Superior than Michigan, ore removed from the Gogebic and Marquette Ranges were shipped out from the ports of Escanaba, causing the latter city to blossom, as well. Setting up in Escanaba was a sound business decision by Seavey, with a growing number of customers for the smaller, but still desirable, cargo he could import. The decade between 1900 and 1910 saw a major population boom for the small northern town, jumping from 9,500 to 13,200 permanent inhabitants.

Karen Lindquist, of the Delta County Historical Society, informs me: "Escanaba was a pretty rough town and this area had a lot of interesting characters. There were over ninety saloons in town in the early 1900s and most were busy. The ore docks, rail yards and lumber camps were filled with a lot of rough characters, and Seavey probably fit right in." This was the last major population increase in the city's history, and its numbers have actually been declining since the 1960s, a phenomenon all too commonplace in the Upper Peninsula.

Although 1910 surpassed 1900 in terms of population, 1907 may have been one of the last outstanding years for the region's economy. A financial panic in 1907–8 caused lake traffic to drop anywhere from 20 to 60 percent, depending on the industry. Timber was being removed faster than the trees could be replaced, and in 1909, one-seventh of Michigan's land was on the delinquent tax list, as the owners simply walked away from the now-barren acres.

These economic troubles were not merely an upper Michigan situation but a widespread concern to just about everybody. A financial crisis took place in the United States over a three-week period starting in mid-October 1907, when the New York Stock Exchange fell almost 50 percent from its peak the previous year. Panic occurred, as this low was already during a time of economic recession and there were numerous runs on banks and trust companies. The 1907 panic eventually spread throughout the nation when many state and local banks and businesses entered bankruptcy. Primary causes of the run included "a reduction of market liquidity" (being able to produce customer's cash) by a number of New York City banks and a loss of confidence among depositors, exacerbated by unregulated side wagers at "bucket shops." At these establishments, rather than trade in stocks directly, a customer could gamble on whether stocks would rise or fall. Bucket shops were made illegal after they were cited as a major contributor to the two stock market crashes in the early 1900s.

The panic was triggered by the failed attempt in October to corner the market on stock of F. Augustus Heinze's newly created United Copper Company (a consolidation of five former copper companies). When this attempt (perpetrated by Heinze's own brother!) failed, banks that had lent money to the cornering scheme suffered runs that later spread to affiliated banks and trusts that were propping up the Heinze-affiliated banks, leading a week later to the downfall of the Knickerbocker Trust Company, New York City's third-largest trust. The collapse of the Knickerbocker spread fear throughout the city's trusts as regional banks withdrew reserves from New York City banks. Panic extended across the nation as vast numbers of people withdrew deposits from their regional banks. Many months would go by before the market began to right itself again, and the Heinze brothers faced legal ramifications. But the damage was done.

The year 1908 started off poorly for Roaring Dan, as well. On March 17, 1908, his son, Earl, died, not yet six years old. He was buried at Holy Cross Cemetery in Escanaba with a very large headstone. This burial adds yet another mystery to the Seavey tale; Holy Cross appears to be a strictly Roman Catholic cemetery, but there is no indication that Seavey was ever a practicing Catholic. Perhaps Zilda Seavey was Catholic, which would answer this question. But the answer would raise more questions in the process. If Zilda was a devoted Catholic, how did she end up marrying a non-Catholic in a non-Catholic ceremony?

There is, ultimately, no indication that either Dan or Zilda Seavey was ever affiliated with a Catholic parish. Tom Stannard of the Marquette

Earl Seavey's headstone
is by far the largest within
several yards. *Author's photo.*

diocese tells me: "As to why they chose a Catholic cemetery is unknown to
me, but it isn't uncommon, especially today, to have non-Catholics buried
here. I don't think they would have been able to tell them no, because that
would probably fall on some type of religious discrimination. It's possible
they may have had other family here who were Catholic and chose the
cemetery for that reason." Earl has the biggest stone for several yards, but no
known family could be discerned.

Not that it was any consolation, but shortly after losing a son, Dan gained
a son-in-law. Seavey's daughter Josephine married Edward C. Ward in
Benzie County, Michigan, in April 1908. We do not know much about Ward,
though William Duchaine wrote: "Dan's own marriage was not allowed to
interfere with his wandering adventures, but that of his daughter concerned
him deeply. Only the best man with his fists was tolerated as a suitor, and this
came to be Ed Ward, the best fighter out of Frankfort." Ward's prowess as a
fighter cannot be confirmed.

4

THE *NELLIE JOHNSON*

I f Seavey had a nemesis, that adversary would be none other than Captain Preston H. Ueberroth and his ship the *Tuscarora*.

Ueberroth was born on October 26, 1862, in Pennsylvania. His parents were Edwin R and Anna Mariah Ueberroth, both Pennsylvania natives. Their ancestry traced back to Hessians—German mercenaries—who came over around the time of the Revolutionary War.

Ueberroth enlisted in the United States Revenue Cutter Service on September 22, 1885, at age twenty-two. Not long after, likely around 1888, he married Marie Glenn Thomas. The couple made their home in Philadelphia, though Preston was rarely around, sometimes sailing as far away as the Pacific coast.

In July 1907, Ueberroth was appointed captain of the USRC *Tuscarora*, replacing Thomas D. Walker, who had reached the mandatory retirement age of sixty-four. The newspapers noted that Ueberroth, at age forty-four, was a "comparatively young man" to lead a crew, making this appointment quite an honor.

The *Tuscarora* had been built in 1901 by the William R. Trigg Company of Richmond, Virginia, and was launched on October 12 of that year. The ship had a displacement of 620 tons, a length of 178 feet and was armed with two Ordnance QF Hotchkiss "six-pounders." Propelled by two Babcock and Wilcox single-ended boilers, one vertical triple-expansion steam engine and one shaft, the *Tuscarora* had a listed cruising speed of 4.2 knots (or 4.8 miles per hour).

On September 21, 1907, the steam screw *Alexander Nimitz* sprang a leak and foundered near Vermillion Point on Lake Superior. The crew attempted to purposely beach the ship, but the pounding weather would not allow any escape. Of the seventeen members of the crew, eleven made it to safety, but six—including Captain John Randall—were lost. Ueberroth and the *Tuscarora* came by a week later to retrieve the body of Captain Randall. Ueberroth spoke to the press when he came in to port, telling them that a full investigation would be launched. The U.S. Life-Saving Service had men stationed at Vermillion Point but appeared to have offered no assistance. Also as a consequence of this failure, the *Tuscarora*'s launch boat was being fitted with a ten-horsepower gasoline engine to better help in future incidents.

In less than a year with Ueberroth at the helm, the *Tuscarora* would meet Seavey and cement his notoriety.

Seavey's most infamous exploit was the hijacking of the schooner *Nellie Johnson*, a forty-ton ship owned by Captain Robert J. McCormick. Some versions of the story say that Seavey had once worked on the ship when the vessel was owned by Captain Pabst. While no record of this has been found, the Seavey-Pabst link is at least plausible from what we have seen. Other accounts say that Seavey himself had owned the ship at one time, though this seems rather unlikely. No record exists to my knowledge to show Seavey having any title on the craft. The official record states that the ship was constructed in 1894 for John Johnson of St. James, on Beaver Island. Next at the helm was Peter Johnson of St. James, likely a son or brother, as recently as 1907. There is no mention of Pabst.

On June 11, 1908, Seavey supposedly came aboard the *Nellie Johnson* in Grand Haven, Michigan, with a large amount of alcohol, which he offered to share with the crew. Once they became intoxicated, Seavey tossed them overboard. Another version of the story has Seavey meeting the crew at a local tavern, where he proceeded to drink them under the table before heading to the dock and stealing the ship.

Either way, Seavey sailed the *Nellie Johnson* to Chicago, where he attempted to sell the cargo of cedar posts. Some sources suggest he was successful, though this does not seem to be the case. No buyer has been named. The U.S. Revenue Cutter Service gave chase in the *Tuscarora*, captained by Preston H. Ueberroth, several days later. Why the delay of an official response? Regardless, Seavey was still on Lake Michigan, and his days were numbered.

Alongside Ueberroth was Deputy Marshal Thomas Harwood Currier, affectionately known as "Big Tom." Currier had been born in New York to Thomas H. Currier Sr. and Phidelia J. Storrs. In the *Tuscarora* logbook for June 22, Third Lieutenant John Farrell McGourty wrote, "Received on board Marshal Thomas Currier and Robert McCormick, master and owner of schooner Nellie Johnson for a cruise to recover his vessel which had been stolen on the 11th."

Prior to enlistment, McGourty had studied law at Yale but evidently felt a maritime career was far more exciting. His parents were both Irish immigrants who initially settled in Massachusetts and later moved to Connecticut, putting him near the academy in New London.

Ueberroth telegraphed the U.S. Treasury Department on June 23: "The men on board the schooner are Daniel Seavey, William Loquist and Hugh Colton, known in Chicago as lawless men. William Loquist has been held for counterfeiting, and although guilty of the crime, was given his freedom upon turning state's evidence." How the names of Seavey's companions were ascertained is unknown.

Colton's lawlessness is unknown to me, but Ueberroth was correct concerning Loquist. He had been arraigned in Chicago on March 7, only a few months prior, on the charge of counterfeiting. Arraigned with him were A.L. McIntosh, A.R. Rothe, William O'Neill, Roscoe Tobias and the latter's sister Inez Tobias Stevens. The Tobias siblings were also leftist radicals, affiliated with the Socialist Party. Another sibling, Mary Tobias Marcy, was well known in her day as a writer and editor for the *International Socialist Review*. Roscoe Tobias would later write a notorious pamphlet titled "Women as Sex Vendors" and was briefly held for the shooting murder of his brother-in-law, anarchist printer Lee Phelan. Tobias made news again when he helped raise bail for "Big Bill" Hayward, the founder of the Industrial Workers of the World (IWW, or Wobblies). Tobias ultimately committed suicide in 1930, leaving a note that read simply, "What I am doing must be done."

Before going too far down this rabbit hole, it should be said that simply because Roscoe and Inez Tobias were radicals does not mean their co-conspirator William Loquist was as well. And even if Loquist was, this does not mean that Seavey was. We have nothing to suggest that Seavey had any political leanings whatsoever. We cannot even say that Seavey was involved in their counterfeiting, despite his former involvement in such things; how he knew Loquist and whether their alliance was for criminal purposes can only be guessed at. This detour aside, let us return to the chase by the *Tuscarora*.

Seavey had moored the *Nellie Johnson* and was again sailing in the *Wanderer*. After several days, he was captured on June 27. First Lieutenant Walker Waller Joynes described the rather mundane event in the log: "At 3:25, stopped and boarded schooner Wanderer of Bay Port, Seavey master.

Frankfort Pier Head Light House bearing NE 7 miles. Had the master come aboard where he was arrested by Deputy U.S. Marshal Thomas Currier of Chicago, on the charge of mutiny and revolt and violation of section 5360 RS (mutiny) and confined him to the brig for safe-keeping. Issued the confined man a ration." Seavey's two companions were not with him at the time of arrest. The Frankfort South Pierhead Light referenced here was nearing the end of its life; the final keeper, Joseph Wilmat, retired in 1911, and the light was dismantled soon after (though some pieces were used in the construction of a more modern light).

The charge of "revolt or mutiny on shipboard" is worded as follows:

> *Whoever, being of the crew of a vessel of the United States, on the high seas, or on any other waters within the admiralty and maritime jurisdiction of the United States, unlawfully and with force, or by fraud, or intimidation, usurps the command of such vessel from the master or other lawful officer in command thereof, or deprives him of authority and command on board, or resists or prevents him in the free and lawful exercise thereof, or transfers such authority and command to another not lawfully entitled thereto, is guilty of a revolt and mutiny, and shall be fined not more than two thousand dollars and imprisoned not more than ten years.*

A careful reading of the law shows a flaw in the charge—such a crime would apply only if Seavey was a member of the crew, which he was not.

Seavey was taken to Chicago in irons, arriving on June 29. At this time, the best-known photograph of Dan Seavey was taken. The newspaper story wired across the country noted that the chase "brings to mind Captain Kidd" and "recalls the stories of piracy on the high seas." Comparisons were made to Walter Scott's novel *The Pirate*. Headlines screamed out to readers with such eye-catching titles as "Wild Chase on the Lake" and trumpeting the "alleged pirate."

According to most newspaper accounts, Seavey was arrested on the charge of "piracy," but as we have seen, he was officially charged with something closer to "unauthorized removal of a vessel on which he had once been a seaman." This actual charge was fortunate, as conviction under the "piracy" law meant the death penalty. He was released on bond.

Preston Ueberroth docked at Milwaukee on June 30 and was met by reporters who wanted to hear firsthand about the exciting adventure being reported by the Chicago newspapers. The captain told them that the *Tuscarora* needed repairs because "the speed of the revenue cutter was so

The iconic photo of Daniel Seavey, as captured by the *Chicago Daily News. Chicago Historical Museum.*

great that the heat of the funnel burned off all the paint." Ueberroth was able to relate the story in his own words.

The chase began with a telephone call, with Ueberroth at Frankfort informing others that he had located the *Nellie Johnson* and *Wanderer* in a river off of Lake Michigan.

> *We had hardly done this* [notified others] *when we sighted the schooner under full sail with a good stiff breeze, sailing directly out into the lake. As we had a good description of Seavey's schooner, the Wanderer, we were certain of our boat and steamed after her. It was an exciting trip. He had a good start, but we fired up and made fast time, with the result that in an hour or two we had caught up with the schooner. We hailed the man and ordered him to heave to. I then sent an armed crew, with their arms concealed, for he was known to be a desperate man, with instructions to bring him aboard.*

Ueberroth continued:

> *This was done, and when he reached our vessel the warrant was read by Marshal Currier and Seavey was put under arrest. The Wanderer was sent back and moored to the wharf at Frankfurt, while the owner of the Nellie Johnson, Captain R.G. McCormick, removed his own schooner to his home. The pirate was surprised, to say the least. He said that we never would have caught him had he had another half hour's start. It was one of the most exciting trips we have had, and the capture kept our crew busy.*

The italics are mine. Note that Ueberroth does not hesitate to refer to Seavey as the "pirate."

While the story carried in many papers made the adventure out to be an exciting chase, the *Sturgeon Bay Advocate* took a more humorous approach on July 2. It noted that Seavey "is quite well known in these parts, and while he does not bear any too good a reputation, he was not thought to be as bad as he has been made to appear by the metropolitan press." The editor bet "dollars to doughnuts" that none of the "desperate pirates" were armed, and joked that while the *Tuscarora* could easily go twenty miles per hour, the *Wanderer* could only do eight "with a hurricane behind her."

On July 7, U.S. commissioner Mark A. Foote (1858–1933) presented the charges to a grand jury, but the charges were later dropped, possibly because Captain McCormick failed to appear for said grand jury, according to some accounts. Richard Boyd says it is "certainly…not the case" that the charges were dropped because McCormick failed to show, but he does not explain why he feels this way. Jacques offers the alternate explanation that Seavey was freed "thanks to the efforts of a good Chicago lawyer, said to have been a good friend of Seavey." No record of the case's dismissal has been found, nor has any attorney been identified by name.

For the rest of his life, Seavey was tagged as a "pirate," though he generally maintained that he won the *Nellie Johnson* in a poker game—a pathetically obvious fabrication. Boyd did conduct a series of searches at the National Archives between 2005 and 2007 and was unable to find Admiralty Court records, U.S. Criminal Court records, hearing dockets for Commissioner Foote or arrest warrants in the U.S. Marshal files. The arrest apparently no longer has any surviving documentation outside of the newspaper accounts.

In the official logbook of the *Tuscarora*, the pursuit and arrest of Roaring Dan are clearly described, and some myths can be dispelled.

First, the log discloses that the gunboat did not burn the paint off her stack during the chase of Seavey; that had occurred several days earlier while the ship steamed north at flank speed. As quoted earlier, Ueberroth told the press that "the speed of the revenue cutter was so great that the heat of the funnel burned off all the paint." This was strictly true, but with the media asking about Seavey, it was clearly implied that this erosion happened during the chase.

And then there is a cannon shot that appears in some retellings. Allegedly, Seavey would not stop his flight until the revenue cutter fired a shot that went over the top of Seavey's ship, informing him of the seriousness. According to Boyd, "Certainly the cannon shot scenario did not occur, because it would have been recorded in the official log. It was likely fabricated by the *Chicago Daily News*, which followed the event closely and first reported it." Boyd is correct on this point; Ueberroth would have mentioned it to reporters if it was true.

In the official record, the *Wanderer* "hove to" as the *Tuscarora* approached. In this sense, "hove to" means his boat came to a standstill and positioned itself to be tied to another craft. Seavey stepped aboard when requested and was summarily arrested by Marshal Currier; no contingent of armed men was involved. Roaring Dan was then placed in the brig and taken to Chicago without incident. What can one conclude from these discrepancies? Clearly, the newspapers enhanced and embellished elements of the event—as was the practice of the time—and Ueberroth did his part to puff up the tale.

Boyd continues: "Moreover, the media may have introduced the idea of piracy. None of the official documents examined actually cites this charge. On the other hand, the now-lost arrest warrant could have listed piracy, but that charge might have been amended at the time of arraignment—a fairly common procedure. Thus, the precise origin of this claim remains unclear." Boyd is wholeheartedly correct on this point, though it appears the "mutiny" charge was firm well before arraignment. Although the Revenue Cutter Service and government in general failed to issue a correction, the branding of Seavey as a pirate was almost entirely a media creation.

For his part, Captain Ueberroth did little to dissuade talk of piracy, beyond what is noted above. And when asked about the case again on October 22, 1908, he told the *Sturgeon Bay Advocate*: "The last I heard from Captain Dan Seavey, he was in jail in Chicago, waiting to be tried for piracy. I had received orders from my superior to capture Seavey and I did it after a long chase over Lake Michigan. I would not enter into any harbor for the purpose of taking him, but I was determined to make the captain on the high seas to avoid any and all complications that might possibly arise." Oddly, you would expect that by October Ueberroth would have known the disposition of the case; surely, he would have been called as a witness.

The *Tuscarora*, incidentally, had its own internal problems during the summer of 1908. One of the crew, a certain Fred Luedke, was assigned to the ship in April and had been a problem from the start. He complained about the discipline and poor-quality food and, finally, in August, jumped overboard and swam to shore, where he walked to an uncle's house. Luedke was tracked through Milwaukee by the U.S. Marshals and was put under arrest by his crew. After a short stay in the same ship jail cell Seavey had recently kept warm, Luedke was court-martialed for desertion. The penalty could have been as high as five years in Leavenworth Prison, the loss of citizenship and the forfeiture of all pay. Luedke apparently got off fairly light; Leavenworth has no record of him spending a single year there.

Commissioner Mark Foote made his place in history not long after the Seavey affair. In December 1908, Foote oversaw the extradition of Latvian radical Christian Ansoff Rudowitz. Though not a household name today, Rudowitz and his case was a big deal at the time. He was defended by the famed Chicago attorney Clarence Darrow and was supported by social activist Jane Addams of Hull House. When Foote ordered Rudowitz deported, Addams successfully rallied enough support to get the order overturned by President Theodore Roosevelt's secretary of state, Elihu Root.

Captain Robert McCormick owned the *Nellie Johnson* for just a single year; by 1909, the ship was in the hands of Harvey Morrison of Traverse City, Michigan. At least one more owner, A.S. Cunningham, would come along before the *Nellie Johnson* was abandoned and fell into disrepair in 1917.

"Big Tom" Currier, the deputy marshal who pursued Seavey on Lake Michigan, passed away in Chicago on December 8, 1910, at age sixty-four. Newspapers across the country ran his obituary and noted his striking resemblance to President William Howard Taft.

World War I was a time of trial and error for the newly formed U.S. Coast Guard, established in January 1915, when the Revenue Cutter Service and the U.S. Life-Saving Service merged. With the entry of the United States into the war on April 6, 1917, the Coast Guard personnel and fleet were officially transferred to the U.S. Navy for the duration of the conflict.

John McGourty, one of the crew who pursued Seavey, met his fate on September 26, 1918. The Coast Guard cutter *Tampa*, sailing alone at dusk, with its silhouette visible against the night sky, was sighted by a German submarine, the *UB-91*, near Milford Haven, Wales. At 8:15 p.m., *UB-91* launched a torpedo that blasted a hole in *Tampa*'s hull in the center of the ship. This was followed by a second explosion, caused either by ignited coal dust or depth charges being detonated as water filled the ship. The *Tampa* sank with all hands—118 Coast Guardsmen, 4 U.S. Navy officers and 16 British passengers—in less than three minutes. There were no witnesses, and the German submarine resurfaced at 8:25 p.m. to look for bodies and debris but found nothing.

W.W. Joynes passed away at age sixty-four in December 1926 while in Antibes, Département des Alpes-Maritimes, Provence-Alpes-Côte d'Azur, France. He reached the rank of lieutenant commander. Why a Coast Guard commander would be in France is unknown; perhaps he stayed behind after the Great War.

Captain Ueberroth would be the last surviving member of the crew that captured Seavey. Within a year of that incident, Ueberroth was transferred to Boston, where he took command of the Revenue Cutter *Gresham*. By 1913, he was "personnel and operations" for the Coast Guard's Revenue Cutter Service, though this apparent desk job did not stop him from sailing. In 1914, he was stationed on the *McCullough* in Unalaska, Alaska, over five thousand miles away from his wife and Philadelphia home. As we have seen, Alaska came to the country's attention during the gold rush, though it is interesting that a Coast Guard ship would patrol its waters forty-five years before statehood. Ueberroth was discharged on October 26, 1926 (at the mandatory age of sixty-four), and he retired with the rank of commodore. He died on May 10, 1933, and is buried in Arlington National Cemetery.

The captain's son, Frank Edwin Preston Ueberroth (1889–1955), followed his father and served his country by sea. Stationed for a while on the battleship *Vermont*, the younger Ueberroth would ultimately become a lieutenant commander and have the honor of being buried in Arlington like his father.

As for the *Tuscarora* itself, it was decommissioned on May 1, 1936, and sold to the Texas Refrigerator Steamship Lines for use as a banana boat. This venture lasted only a few years before the ship was sold for scrap in 1939 to the Boston Iron & Metal Company of Baltimore, Maryland. Where the pieces ended up, we can only imagine.

5

POST-PIRACY ESCAPADES

The August 15, 1908 edition of the *Door County Democrat* reported that Dan Seavey was "touring Lake Michigan with one of the toughest crews he has ever traveled with." Seavey himself was called "a very tough customer" and "hard to kill." According to the article, he allegedly was set free from Chicago after his preliminary hearing on the mutiny charge, but the paper felt no need to expound on the matter.

Instead, it noted how, in early August, Seavey was caught with passengers named Charles Morris, Helen Morris and Pearl Cannon. Some reports give the Morris surname as "Harris." Exactly what was going on aboard the ship is left to the imagination, but on docking in Van's Harbor, Undersheriff Marc Pepin brought them all in for "gross lewdness" and "lascivious behavior." When brought before Judge Oscar Valentine Linden (1860–1929), they were fined twenty-five dollars each on the condition that they leave the district immediately. Linden, the son of Swedish immigrants and a former merchant-turned-politician, was a pioneer in Michigan's Progressive Party. When he attempted a run for statewide office later in life, he ran as a "Bull Moose" in the style of Theodore Roosevelt.

Escanaba's *Iron Port* newspaper was more colorful in its coverage, explaining that Seavey was found on August 6 near Garden with some "soiled doves" (prostitutes). This was "much to the discomfort of many of the citizens." Seavey's "old tricks" were "too well known" to the newspaper subscribers, the editor claimed. Indeed, "those who know Seavey best are of the belief that he is beyond redemption and would find delight in doing wrong, even though it was as easy to walk the straight and narrow path." The article continued on, not mincing words. "Dan and his associates were not living within the bounds of decency or trying to persuade others to do so, but on the contrary were violating the laws of God and man." The residents of Garden would have to "free themselves of the obnoxious quantity."

The *Door County Democrat* article also reported a fight that happened on August 1 in Fayette between Seavey and an unnamed farmer. The men went at each other with billiard cues. Allegedly, Seavey was cut four inches on the back of his head and five inches across the forehead but refused medical attention and wrapped up his wounds with court plaster. After these incidents, a low profile was kept for a year.

Albert Gould, twenty-five, of Garden stopped in Escanaba on June 22, 1909, on his way to Watersmeet in order to take a position with the William Bonifas Lumber Company. Wandering the north shore docks, he ran into Seavey, who asked Gould, "Are you a fisherman?" Gould replied that he was, and Seavey tossed the man into the water. Gould had been "looking on the wine when it was red" and did not swim well at all. Seavey grabbed him

When sailing in to Fayette, Seavey would be greeted by this imposing iron-ore smelting factory. *Author's photo.*

by the hair and pulled him back on the dock. Supervisor Wesley J. Gray of Garden, a farmer by day, heard about the incident and paid for Gould to spend the night in the Globe Hotel. Gray, incidentally, had formerly been associated with Van's Harbor, discussed earlier in our story. He worked as a teamster for Lewis Van Winkle, bringing in groceries for the company store. An oft-repeated tale concerning Gray has him bringing a sleigh full of beer to the mill town when the ice he was driving over collapsed because warm waste water was entering the bay at that point. The beer was salvaged, but a freezing, urine-soaked Gray never lived down his blunder.

Over the winter of 1909–10, Seavey was in Frankfurt, manufacturing and selling "cedar floats," what we typically call fishing bobbers. He was also busy remodeling the cabin on his schooner *Harvey Ransom*. This is the first mention of the *Ransom*, so we can assume he recently acquired the vessel. The previous owner was the Norwegian Erick Lunde, and the only account of the sale states that Lunde "did not make a very good bargain. He was dealing with Dan Seavey, who was a very persuasive man." The *Harvey Ransom* was built in South Haven, Michigan, in 1887, and its port was originally listed as Milwaukee. The schooner was fifty-nine-feet long. At the same time as the remodeling, Seavey was trying to sell off a forty-five-foot gasoline boat with an eleven-foot beam. Seavey swore it was good "for fishing or freighting….All ready for business."

Around 1912, Seavey married for the third time, to one Anne Bradley. She was the daughter of Huron "Henry" Bradley and Caroline Hogarty of Little Harbor, a small logging community on the Garden Peninsula. Huron, furthermore, was the son of legendary Door County figure Allen Bradley, known as the "Giant of Hedgehog Harbor" or the "Gills Rock Giant." Hedgehog Harbor was the former name of the area now known as Gills Rock, on the very tip of the Door Peninsula.

Allen Bradley was famous for his purported feats of strength, such as being able to carry men around simply by having them hang from his beard. This stunt earned him a place in Ripley's Believe it or Not! Bradley had "hands as broad as shovels and was obliged to wear moccasins because no shoes could be bought that were big enough." The locals claimed he could cut seven cords of wood in a single day, which was quite a feat in the days when the crosscut saw was not yet in use and an axe was the tool of choice. Bradley lived off the land, feasting on fish, deer and bear, and he made his clothes from their skins. He was said to be able to lift a log that would usually require six men and could easily stack three-hundred-pound barrels as high as the day is long. While serving in the Civil War, Bradley was taken prisoner by the Confederates. When he found himself alone with only two guards, he picked them up by their necks "like two squirming kittens" and carried them back behind Union lines.

In fact, Allen Bradley was alive and well in Door County when Seavey married Anne, and these two legendary men may have crossed paths. Getting back to Anne, she apparently found Dan to be a better husband than had his two previous wives, as she remained with him until her passing.

6

THE GREAT LAKES STORM OF 1913

Though not every year, the Great Lakes are susceptible to what is called the November Witch, a series of strong winds that frequently blow across the Great Lakes in late autumn. The "witches" are caused by intense low atmospheric pressure over the Great Lakes pulling cold Canadian and Arctic air from the north and warm Gulf of Mexico air from the south. When these cold and warm air masses collide, they can result in hurricane-force winds that stir up large waves on the lakes. Over a century ago, the worst "witch" came in the form of the Great Lakes Storm of 1913.

The Great Lakes Storm of 1913, also known as the Big Blow, was the deadliest and most destructive natural disaster to hit the lakes in recorded history and remains so today. The Great Lakes Storm killed more than 250 people, destroyed nineteen ships and stranded nineteen others. The financial loss in vessels alone was nearly $5 million (roughly $129.3 million in today's dollars). This included about $1 million at current value in lost cargo totaling about 68,300 tons, including such essentials as coal, iron ore and grain.

The storm was first noticed on Thursday, November 6, on the western side of Lake Superior north of Duluth, moving rapidly toward northern Lake Michigan. The weather forecast in the *Detroit News* called for "moderate to brisk" winds for the Great Lakes, with occasional rains Thursday night or Friday for the upper lakes (except on southern Lake Huron), and fair to unsettled conditions for the lower lakes.

On Friday, the weather forecast in the *Times-Herald* of Port Huron, Michigan (retroactively identified as the "standard bearer" in storm coverage), described the storm as "moderately severe." By then, the storm was centered over the upper Mississippi Valley (essentially Minnesota and Wisconsin) and had caused moderate to brisk southerly winds with warmer weather over the lakes. The forecast predicted increased winds and falling temperatures over the next twenty-four hours.

At 10:00 a.m., Coast Guard stations and U.S. Department of Agriculture (USDA) Weather Bureau offices at Lake Superior ports raised white pennants above square red flags with black centers, indicating a storm warning with northwesterly winds. The weather bureau, under the USDA, was later renamed the National Weather Service (NWS) and put under the Department of Commerce. Today, the NWS is under the umbrella of the National Oceanic and Atmospheric Administration (NOAA).

By late afternoon, the storm signal flags were replaced with a vertical sequence of red, white and red lanterns, indicating that a hurricane with winds over seventy-four miles per hour (mph) was coming. (The word *hurricane* today usually refers to a tropical cyclone, but traditionally the term was used by meteorologists for any winds over seventy-four mph or, in other words, Force 12 winds on the Beaufort scale. The scale does not exceed 12; most of us would prefer a Force 3 wind, categorized as a "gentle breeze.") The winds on Lake Superior had already reached fifty miles per hour, and an accompanying blizzard was moving toward Lake Huron. Because weather forecasting was quite primitive (as we will see), many sailors considered the predictions a "coin flip" and did not take them seriously.

By Saturday, the storm's status had been upgraded to "severe." The storm was centered over eastern Lake Superior, covering the entire area of the lake. The weather forecast of the *Port Huron Times-Herald* stated that southerly winds had remained "moderate to brisk." Northwesterly winds had reached gale strength on northern Lake Michigan and western Lake Superior, with winds of up to sixty mph at Duluth.

A false lull in the storm, called a "sucker hole" by sailors, came next. This short span of good weather "suckered" sailors into leaving port just in time for a storm to resume at full force. This false sense of security allowed traffic to begin flowing again, both down the St. Marys River (where the UP meets Canada) and up Lake Erie, and the Detroit and St. Clair Rivers (that divide the Detroit area from Ontario), into Lake Huron. Gale wind flags were raised at more than one hundred ports but were ignored by many ship captains, who believed the worst was over. Long ships traveled all that day

The flag used by the
U.S. Coast Guard to
designate strong winds.
Wikicommons.

through the St. Marys River, all night through the Straits of Mackinac and
early Sunday morning up the Detroit and St. Clair Rivers.

By noon Sunday, weather conditions on lower Lake Huron were close to
normal for a November gale. Barometric pressures in some areas began to
rise, bringing hope of an end to the storm. The low-pressure area that had
moved across Lake Superior was moving northeast, away from the lakes.

The U.S. Weather Bureau had issued the first of its twice-daily reports
at approximately 8:00 a.m.; the bureau did not send another report to
Washington, D.C., until 8:00 p.m. This proved to be a serious problem. The
storm would have the better part of a day to build up hurricane forces before
the bureau headquarters in Washington would have detailed information.
In the days of one newspaper per day and no such thing as television, there
was no concept of "up to the minute" news and weather. The first TV
weatherman, George Cowling, did not appear until 1954.

Along southeastern Lake Erie, near the city of Erie, Pennsylvania,
a southern low-pressure area was moving toward the lake. This low had
formed overnight and was therefore absent from Friday's weather map.
It had been traveling northward and began moving northwestward after
passing over Washington, D.C.

In Buffalo, morning northwest winds had shifted to northeast by noon
and were blowing southeast by 5:00 p.m., with the fastest gusts, eighty mph,
occurring between 1:00 p.m. and 2:00 p.m. Just 180 miles to the southwest, in

Cleveland, winds remained northwest during the day, shifting to the west by 5:00 p.m. and maintaining speeds of more than fifty mph. The fastest gust in Cleveland, seventy-nine mph, occurred at 4:40 p.m. There was a dramatic drop in barometric pressure at Buffalo, from 29.52 inches of mercury (inHg) at 8:00 a.m. to 28.77 inHg at 8:00 p.m.

The rotating low continued along its northward path into the evening, bringing its counterclockwise winds in harmony with the northwesterly winds already hitting Lakes Superior and Huron. This resulted in an explosive increase in northerly wind speeds and swirling snow. Ships on Lake Huron that were south of Alpena, Michigan—especially around Harbor Beach and Port Huron in Michigan and Goderich and Sarnia in Ontario, in the water between the Michigan Thumb and Canada—were battered with massive waves moving southward toward the St. Clair River.

Some ships had sought shelter along the coast in Michigan or along the Goderich to Point Edward coast, presumably shallower and less susceptible to large waves, but few survived the powerful north winds. Three of the larger ships were found upside down, leaving no doubt of the extremely high winds and, indeed, unbearably tall waves.

From 8:00 p.m. to midnight, the storm became what modern meteorologists call a "weather bomb" (more technically "explosive cyclogenesis") indicating a massive drop of atmospheric pressure within twenty-four hours. Sustained hurricane-speed winds of more than seventy miles per hour ravaged the four western lakes. The worst damage was done on Lake Huron, as numerous ships scrambled for shelter along its southern end. Gusts of ninety miles per hour were reported off Harbor Beach, Michigan. The lake's shape allowed northerly winds to increase unchecked, because of the lower surface friction of water compared to land and the wind following the lake's length.

In retrospect, weather forecasters of the time did not have enough data or understanding of atmospheric interactions to predict or comprehend the events of Sunday, November 9. Frontal mechanisms, referred to then as "squall lines," were not yet understood. In meteorology jargon, a squall line is known as a "quasi-linear convective system," which simply means a line of thunderstorms forming along or ahead of a cold front. As noted, surface observations were collected only twice daily at stations around the country, and by the time this data was collected and hand-drawn maps created, the information released lagged actual weather conditions by hours.

One ship captain made it to Port Huron at this time, his vessel flooded and ice-encrusted and its windows shattered. He said (correctly) that this was "the

The remnants of a life-saving station in Michigan following the Great Storm of 1913. *Library of Congress.*

worst storm to my knowledge that has ever swept the Great Lakes." Another man told the local newspaper bluntly: "Bodies of many sailors are drifting in the lake, but the government has removed the means of recovering them. Instead the corpses will drift with the wind until thrown up on the beach, as a score already have been. They may lie in the sands in some deserted place and rot for all the aid the government gives."

On Monday morning, the storm had moved northeast of London, Ontario, dragging lake-effect blizzards in its wake. An additional seventeen inches of snow were dumped on Cleveland that day, filling the streets with snowdrifts six feet high. Streetcar operators stayed with their stranded, powerless vehicles for two nights, eating whatever food was provided by local residents. Travelers were forced to take shelter and wait for things to clear. One such traveler was Helen Keller, in town to give a lecture. She described the storm from her hotel room by saying, "The storm waves, like sound waves or the waves of the wireless, will not be deterred by stone walls and plate glass windows."

Along the shoreline, blizzards shut down traffic and communication, causing hundreds of thousands of dollars in damage. A grand total twenty-two-inch snowfall in Cleveland put stores out of business for two days. After the final blizzards hit Cleveland, the city was paralyzed under feet of ice and snow and was without power for days. Telephone poles had been broken, and power cables lay in tangled masses.

By Tuesday, the storm was rapidly moving across eastern Canada. Without the warm lake waters, the winds lost strength quickly. This also meant less snowfall, both because of the fast motion of the storm and the lack of lake-effect snow. All shipping was halted on Monday and part of Tuesday along the St. Lawrence River around Montreal.

There were four-foot snowdrifts around Lake Huron. Power was out for several days across Michigan and Ontario, cutting off telephone and telegraph communications. A recently completed $100,000 Chicago breakwater, intended to protect the Lincoln Park basin from storms, was swept away in a few hours. The Milwaukee harbor lost its entire south breakwater and much of the surrounding area that had been recently renovated.

The greatest damage was done on the lakes. Major shipwrecks occurred on all but Lake Ontario, with most happening on southern and western Lake Huron. Those in the know recounted that waves reached at least thirty-five feet in height. Being shorter in length than waves ordinarily formed by gales, they occurred in rapid succession, with three waves frequently striking one after another. Early meteorologists also stated that the wind often blew in directions opposite to the waves below. This was the result of the storm's cyclonic motion, a phenomenon rarely seen on the Great Lakes.

The storm had several long-term consequences. Complaints against the U.S. Weather Bureau of alleged unpreparedness resulted in increased efforts to achieve more accurate weather forecasting and faster realization and communication of proper storm warnings. Though, it is worth noting that the bureau refused to accept that the great loss of life was in any way its fault or that it shirked their responsibility. One representative said, "Daring disregard of government storm signals are the main causes of the latest disasters on the Great Lakes." Another representative concurred. "The department will refuse absolutely to take any responsibility for the acts of vessel owners or captains in ignoring the warnings, shown by the records to have been issued in advance of the storm."

Criticism of the shipping companies and shipbuilders led to a series of discussions with insurers and seasoned sailors to seek safer designs for vessels. This resulted in the construction of ships with greater stability and strength. Immediately following the blizzard of Cleveland, the city began a campaign to move all utility cables underground, in tubes beneath major streets. The project took half a decade but greatly reduced the vulnerability of city infrastructure.

According to Dr. Richard Boyd, Seavey was in the great storm aboard his boat the *Harvey Ransom*. On board were Mark Ward of Garden, laborer

Albert Clifton of Fayette and Seavey's brother-in-law Elmer Ellsworth of Little Harbor. They were delivering hay to Fayette Harbor. With the storm raging, the ship took refuge in Sac Bay under the Burnt Bluff. Hullie Dalgard, described in the newspaper as a "Fayette oldtimer," explained what happened next. "Seavey was a daring man and everything would have been all right if the *Ransom* had not come down on top of a broken off pound net stake. The stake rammed through her hull and ripped her wide open so the water poured in. The *Ransom* was doomed. Seavey and his crew took to a small boat and made the safety of the rocky shore." A reporter from Escanaba eventually found the wreckage in 1949.

Boyd notes that a compass belonging to Seavey is in the Garden historical museum. The instrument was donated by commercial fisherman Royal "Bud" Tallman (1927–2013) of Manistique in 1982. Tallman said the compass had been given to his father in exchange for some unidentified service. Boyd believes the compass came from the *Harvey Ransom*.

While the 1913 storm remains the worst on record, November storms remained deadly for decades to come, even as ships became bigger and, presumably, more sturdy, and as weather forecasting improved. The most famous ship to sink was no doubt the freighter *Edmund Fitzgerald* on November 10, 1975. At the time of its construction, the ship was the largest on the Great Lakes, but this did not prevent the storm from taking the lives of all twenty-nine crewmen.

7

THE SAWMILL FIRE

Tragedy seemed to follow Seavey wherever he went. Indeed, some of his misfortune (e.g., the *Nellie Johnson*) was of his own making, but he lost a small fortune in Alaska, met disastrous ends on the water and his own family was irrevocably fractured. The spring of 1915 brought with it more chaos and untimely death.

Early reports from the Associated Press were brief and tragic. In no uncertain terms, Dan Seavey was said to have "burned to death at Fayette" while "his companion" James Broady "was drowned at Escanaba." Seavey "was widely known as a pilot and an eccentric character." His body "has been taken to Escanba." Like much of Dan's life, this report of his death was a bit of an exaggeration, and his body made it to Escanaba very much alive, though the situation was indeed fatal.

The official story soon came out that James Broady (1895–1915) and Lucas Mercier (1889–1915) spent the day, May 29, 1915, loading up saws, engines and other machines aboard the 117-foot schooner the *RP Mason*, sometimes described as a lumber barge. The ship was specifically built for the lumber trade on Lake Michigan, all the way back in 1868 by Harrison C. Pierson. With over forty-five years on the lake, the *Mason* had seen a few things, including the deaths of three crewmen in the Mackinac Straits.

Seavey, who helped load the ship for a while, went to take a nap. Around midnight, with Seavey still asleep, a fire broke out in the sawmill attached to Seavey's home on Garden Bay. According to Seavey, the smoke was overtaking his room when Broady came in to wake him up. The blaze was too intense to leave the house normally, so Seavey jumped out the window, knocking himself unconscious for two hours. He did not deny that he had been drinking, which may have made his escape less graceful. Rescuers, including Broady's brother Robert, who saw the fire, came to help get Broady out, but Broady had trapped himself in the heroics. The *Escanaba Daily Mirror* reported that Broady's "charred, unrecognizable body was dug out of the ruins, the lower limbs entirely burned off and the head and arms mere pieces of charred bones."

Despite being in the water, the *RP Mason* also burned. Mercier, who was part owner of the property with Seavey, saw the fire spread from the mill to the dock and on to the ship and tried to push the boat away from the burning dock. He was evidently unsuccessful and fell into the water and drowned. The newspapers said Mercier had been drinking that day, which likely contributed to his poor swimming ability. The burned property was estimated to be a $7,500 loss. A certain Dr. Hughes arrived to treat Seavey's burns, and Hughes called Dr. George Casper Bartley (1884–1941), the coroner and a noted surgeon in Escanaba.

Local rumors accused Seavey himself of starting the fire and killing his associates, particularly Broady, though no reason was given. Did people think Seavey would resort to murder for simple insurance fraud? Sheriff Andrew Iverson and District Attorney Herbert J. Rushton went to Gouley's Bay to question witnesses. In doing so, Seavey was cleared of any wrongdoing. "Dan Seavey's story was truthful, as far as I can determine," Iverson told the press.

Coroner Bartley assembled a quick jury for an inquest, and at Garden the following men were present: R.A. McDonald, Harry J. Green, David Gray, John Coleman, Con Dolgard and farm laborer Rupert J. Green. They gave the verdict of "accidental death" for both Broady and Mercier.

More specifically, they ruled that "James Broady lost his life May 30 at midnight by accidental means, having perished in attempting to save the life of a fellow being from a burning building. Location of this accident was Gouley's Bay, a point five miles south and east from Garden Village." Meanwhile, "Lucius Mercier met his death by accidental means having fell into the water at Gouley's Bay…and being unable to swim or in any other way aid himself drowned." In short, the story told by Seavey was now on the record as the definitive explanation.

A quick aside here. Those who don't spend a great deal of time digging into historical deaths may not be familiar with coroner inquests. A holdover from centuries of English tradition, an inquest was the manner of determining death when the cause wasn't obviously natural. The coroner (a representative of the crown—*coroner* literally means "a man of the crown") and an assortment of men would visit the body and decide the cause of death. This system was often corrupt, and even more often incompetent. No member of the jury was a law enforcement officer, and very rarely did anyone have medical knowledge. Studies done in the cities of New York and Boston in the early 1900s found a plethora of nonsensical causes of death on death certificates and some clear cases of homicide overlooked for political reasons.

Delta County, to its credit, was apparently ahead of its time. Coroner Bartley was a licensed doctor and trained surgeon and would be able to examine bodies in a more professional and precise manner if need be. Coroner, being an elected position, meant there was no medical requirement. Today, while most counties still have a coroner, death investigations are almost always handled by a medical examiner specifically trained in pathology and able to perform autopsies.

Seavey was resting at St. Francis Hospital when a reporter came to interview him. "Are you Dan Seavey, the man they call a pirate?" he was asked. Seavey replied: "I'm the man, but this talk of piracy is all a joke. There is nothing to it. I was an officer of the United States government and was doing my duty when people thought I was a pirate." The reporter wrote that despite his "rugged life," Seavey was "quite good to look upon." While we have already noted that at various points in his life Seavey may have worked for the navy, the Bureau of Indian Affairs or the U.S. Marshals, there is no reason to believe he held any of these positions during the *Nellie Johnson* hijacking, and he was flatly lying to the reporter.

The sawmill rumors refused to die, forcing prosecutor Herbert J. Rushton (1877–1947) and Sheriff Iverson to return on June 11 and spend two full days investigating the scene and searching for answers. Reporters spoke to Seavey again, who told them: "I want to be vindicated and you can say that any investigation is welcomed. That cloud of suspicion hanging over me will have to be cleared up and any investigation towards the settlement of those rumors meets with my approval."

Two weeks after the fire, one John S. Mills (born 1861) was charged with arson. Mills, a forty-year resident of Delta County, was boarding at Mary Gouley's place on Garden Bluff at the time, and he will reappear in our story later. The newspaper suspected "bad blood" between Mills and Seavey; this does not seem to be correct, based on my knowledge of the pair, and Mills hired attorney Henry Robert Dotsch to help him set the record straight.

Druggist Roy Kuehn was also arrested for selling alcohol on a Sunday (a violation of state law), following a warrant from DA Rushton. Kuehn was alleged to have supplied liquor to the sawmill crew, thus indirectly leading to the tragedy. How the authorities were able to trace liquor to Kuehn, and confirm it was a Sunday sale, is unknown, but the evidence was clearly there, because the charge stuck. Mills was later released, while Kuehn served sixty days.

On July 13, 1915, the county board met and paid people for their role in the investigation. Each of the jurors from the coroner's inquest was given $1.50. Witnesses were also given $1.50 each, including both Dan and Anna Seavey. The other witnesses were Carl Mallinger, Thomas Isabell, Pearl Purdy, John Nolan, John S. Mills and Robert Broady. What role some of these witnesses played is not known.

Rushton used his time as prosecutor as a stepping-stone to bigger things. He was a member of the Michigan state senate from 1927 to 1932 and served as a delegate to the Republican National Convention in 1932 and 1936. In 1927, Rushton drafted the bill that would create the Upper Peninsula State Fair, his most noteworthy piece of legislation. Rushton was a candidate for U.S. representative from Michigan's Eleventh District in 1936 and was elected Michigan state attorney general from 1941 to 1944 before retiring.

Solby LaFave (1872–1948) of Fayette, the caretaker for A.C. Hoy's estate at Garden Bluff, had taken it upon himself to get the sunken vessel *R.P. Mason* brought to the surface and hauled away years later, in March 1938, Hoy was an attorney at Wheaton, Illinois, and did not want a sunken boat near his property. He believed the shore would be better suited for swimming without the shipwreck there. LaFave intended to use 350 empty oil barrels in order to float the 125-foot ship to the surface.

Speaking to the press, LaFave called Seavey his friend and said of him: "Seavey was probably more accused than guilty, and people painted him a lot worse than he actually was. He had a redeeming streak of good nature displayed to a rare few who understood him." Despite LaFave speaking in the past tense, Seavey would end up outliving LaFave. The latter was remembered for his habit of dressing as Santa Claus, even in the summer, and giving out spare change to children. The newspapers said that beyond children, he "was also very kind to all dumb animals."

Josephine Seavey-Ward remarried, to railroad switchman Ernest Patrick Beauchamp of Iron Mountain, on September 2, 1915, at Corunna, Shiawassee County, Michigan (in the dead center of the state, nowhere near the water). The service was done by Justice of the Peace Hugh M. Nichols. Beauchamp came from a long line of French Canadians on both sides of his family, including notable fur traders going back centuries. Was Dan Seavey at this ceremony? He probably was not.

Seavey purchased the Ford River mill and tramways from Harry Rubinsky of Muskegon in August 1916. Ford River is a town just south of Escanaba, on the river of the same name. The plan was to raze the property and sell the material as scrap. Indeed, by September, Seavey was posting classified ads offering ten thousand cords of "short wood and edgings" for sale at "very reasonable" prices. He also requested "smaller vessels" to reach out to him in order to help move the wood. Sales were apparently slow, as the same classified ad appeared in the Sturgeon Bay newspaper through at least February 1917.

8

THE *JAMES H. HALL*

It goes without saying that shipbuilding has existed for as long as there have been ships. No doubt men were traveling, fishing and exploring even before the days of Noah. Yet, like any trade, the construction of ships improved over time, and it would serve us well to understand the modern era of shipbuilders, so central to our story.

The "modern" era of shipbuilding emerged only about 250 years ago, relatively recent in the grand scheme of things. The Industrial Revolution made possible the use of new materials and designs that radically altered shipbuilding. Iron was gradually adopted in ship construction, initially in discrete areas in a wood hull requiring greater strength (e.g., deck knees, hanging knees, knee riders and other sharp joints, ones in which a curved, progressive joint could not be achieved). A "knee," in nautical terms, is an angled piece of wood or metal frame used to connect and support the beams and timbers of a ship. Following the knees, in the form of plates riveted together and made watertight, iron was used to form the hull itself.

Sailing-ship technology vastly improved during the early Industrial Revolution (between 1760 and 1825), as "the risk of being wrecked for Atlantic shipping fell by one third, and of foundering by two thirds, reflecting improvements in seaworthiness and navigation respectively." The improvements in seaworthiness have been credited to "replacing the traditional stepped deck ship with stronger flushed decked ones derived from Indian designs, and the increasing use of iron reinforcement." The design originated from Bengal rice ships—the Indian region of Bengal was famous for its shipbuilding industry at the time. One study found that there were considerable improvements in ship speed from 1750 to 1850.

> *We find that average sailing speeds of British ships in moderate to strong winds rose by nearly a third. Driving this steady progress seems to be continuous evolution of sails and rigging, and improved hulls that allowed a greater area of sail to be set safely in a given wind. By contrast, looking at every voyage between the Netherlands and East Indies undertaken by the Dutch East India Company from 1595 to 1795, we find that journey time fell only by ten percent, with no improvement in the heavy mortality, averaging six percent per voyage, of those aboard.*

You read that correctly: in the fifteenth and sixteenth centuries, 6 percent of passengers died on any given voyage.

Initially copying wood construction traditions with a frame over which the hull was fastened, English engineer Isambard Kingdom Brunel's (1806–1859) SS *Great Britain* of 1843 was the first radical new design, being built entirely of wrought iron. Despite its success, and the great savings in cost and space provided by the iron hull, compared to a copper sheathed counterpart, there remained problems with fouling due to the adherence of weeds and barnacles. *Fouling* is the technical term for a buildup of things that attach to something, hindering its usefulness. Here, of course, fouling means barnacles, but it could also be used to describe gunk that builds up in a pipe until it is unable to drain.

As a result, composite construction remained the dominant approach when fast ships were required, with wood timbers laid over an iron frame (*Cutty Sark* is a famous example). Later, *Great Britain*'s iron hull was sheathed in wood to enable the ship to carry a copper-based sheathing. Brunel's *Great Eastern* represented the next great development in shipbuilding, a vessel an unheard-of seven hundred feet long and capable of holding four thousand passengers. Built in association with Scottish civil engineer John Scott Russell (1808–1882), the vessel used what are called "longitudinal stringers" for strength, inner and outer hulls and bulkheads to form multiple watertight compartments. The project was plagued with a number of problems. Russell put in a bid which was far too low, with the result that he was bankrupt halfway through, though he recovered to finish the job. He was a great scientist (pioneering steam travel, study of the Doppler effect and more), but not a particularly smart businessman. Steel also supplanted wrought iron when it became readily available in the latter half of the nineteenth century,

The legendary ship *Cutty Sark. Library of Congress.*

providing great savings when compared with iron in cost and weight. Wood continued to be favored for the decks.

When it comes to Lake Michigan, the true shipbuilding center was on the middle of the Wisconsin shore in Manitowoc, still considered a giant in maritime activities.

In 1863, while the United States was in the midst of the Civil War, Henry Burger, twenty-four, moved north from his home in Milwaukee to Manitowoc, at that time a small community on the western shore of Lake Michigan. There, he married Mary Esslinger, the daughter of a prominent German businessman, and formed the H. Burger Shipyard to produce small, twenty- to thirty-foot Mackinaw fishing boats for local commercial fishermen. His expertise and passion for building extremely high-quality vessels quickly became known throughout the Great Lakes.

Between 1866 and 1869, Henry and his small group of boatbuilders constructed and launched several vessels, including the scow *Menomonee* and the schooners *Fleet Wing* and *S.A. Wood*, making a name for themselves.

In 1870, during the heyday of wood sailing ships, Burger and Greene S. Rand (another Manitowoc pioneer) consolidated their Lake Michigan shipyards to form the Rand and Burger Shipyard, building, among many others, the schooners *City of Manitowoc* and *J.I. Case*. Rand, described as "a big man with a small goatee, sharp eyes and a ready smile," was the company manager, and Burger was the junior partner. This alliance continued until Rand's death in 1885.

In 1886, Henry took his nephew George B. Burger into partnership, forming the Burger and Burger Shipyard. In 1887, envisioning the decline of new wood sailing ships, they purchased the only dry dock in Manitowoc to begin a ship-repair business. A dry dock, as the name implies, is a place to dock boats outside of the water so repairs can be made on them, especially on the rarely handled bottom side.

In 1888, the Burger yard launched the *Lizzie Metzner*, an 80-foot, three-masted schooner built of blue oak. That same year, the 171-foot steamer *Petosky* was launched, defying all superstitions about Fridays being unlucky days for boats. The keel was laid on a Friday, it was launched on a Friday and its maiden voyage was on a Friday. The *Petosky* was very successful but finally met with ill fate in 1935, when it was destroyed by fire in Sturgeon Bay while being converted into a barge.

In 1889, Burger launched the *Cora A*, the last full-rigged schooner built on the Great Lakes. The following year, Burger built and launched the 201-foot ferry *Indiana* for the Goodrich Transportation Company, the largest and by far the most successful passenger steamship company on the Great Lakes. If you have not heard of Goodrich—no relation to the tire manufacturer—this is because it went bankrupt and collapsed in 1933.

The combination of new construction and ship repair was the formula that made Burger prosperous during the 1890s, when many other shipyards struggled. As there were no dry docks between Detroit, Michigan, and Manitowoc, Wisconsin, and none on Lake Superior whatsoever, the Burger shipyard had a steady stream of customers, with eight to ten ships waiting to come in for repairs at any given time.

The company also maintained a large wrecking tug, the *John Gregory*, that often brought in profitable repair jobs. The yard boasted a 337-foot graving dock that could handle vessels of 2,000 tons. *Graving dock* is an alternative name for *dry dock* that is rarely used anymore. The word *graving* is an obsolete nautical term for the scraping, cleaning, painting or tarring of any underwater part of a ship. In addition, Burger had a set of boxes that would lift vessels of 350 tons and a large stock of spars and a spar derrick. A spar in this case refers to a thick pole that could be used for a ship's mast. Between 1870 and the turn of the century, the Burger brand name appeared on almost one hundred new vessels, including steamers, tugs, scows, schooners and barges.

Without question, the Burger name was synonymous with quality and craftsmanship. But it was not alone in Manitowoc.

In 1858, Hans M. Scove moved to Manitowoc and, ten years later, joined the shipyard of Jasper Hanson. Together, the two were a force to

An example of a spar derrick. *National Archives.*

be reckoned with, employing seventy-five men in the construction of many crafts throughout Manitowoc and Two Rivers. During the Civil War, Scove assisted in building the fleet that was sent down the Mississippi River and took part in the capture of Vicksburg in 1863. He was married to Lena Burger, perhaps not coincidentally a member of the Burger shipbuilding family.

Scove had also been instrumental in the construction of a sawmill at Lily Bay. Even regular visitors to Door County are unlikely familiar with Lily Bay, so let's take a slight detour.

In the latter years of the nineteenth century, an estimated eighty-five to one hundred people lived and worked in the little community of Lily Bay. There were, at one time, as many as fifteen buildings in the village, including a post office, store, sawmill, cooper shop, blacksmith shop, boardinghouse and several family homes. In the course of a few years, several industries prospered and vanished, one after another.

One of the first things the settlers did was to build a pier. In those days, piers were a one-third to a half-mile long, with an area at the end large enough for a horse-drawn wagon to turn around. The creek was dammed to raise the water level five feet to facilitate getting logs out. For many years, until the ship canal opened in 1882, the pier at Lily Bay was Sturgeon Bay's major port—an excellent site in the summer and one of the last bays to freeze in the winter.

Canadian Joseph Smith—often called "The Cedar King of Door County"—was the first lumber baron to establish a business in the area. In 1879, he shipped seventy shiploads of cedar worth about $150,000. In fact, what later became Lily Bay was first named St. Joseph in his honor. Kewaunee banker Victor Mashek, who also owned a fleet of schooners, became interested in the area and in 1883 bought out Smith's share of the lumber business. Mashek purchased two thousand acres of timberland in the area of Lily Bay, where he constructed a shingle mill, and another two thousand acres near Clark Lake, between Whitefish Bay and Jacksonport.

Mashek, who had visions of Lily Bay becoming a thriving suburb of Sturgeon Bay, often sailed from Kewaunee to keep an eye on his business ventures, one of which brought about a major change in the lumber industry. He had crews of forty men in the woods cutting hemlock trees and stripping the bark, which was shipped to Chicago to be used in tanning hides. Whereas the hemlock logs had previously been left to rot in the forest, they were now turned into railroad ties, for which there was a booming market in the Midwest.

Mashek's logging crews worked throughout the cold months, with sawmill crews arriving in the spring. The log-sawing men earned fifty dollars a month; the cook, twenty-five dollars; and woodchoppers, fifteen to twenty dollars. The system worked well for a half-dozen years or so, until most of the trees in the Lily Bay area had been cut. This was hastened by the development of the "rake," an addition to the crosscut saws that had replaced axes for felling trees. While the horizontal saws were a definite improvement, sawdust quickly filled the cut, causing the saw to jam and slowing the process. The rake, with a short tooth added to the saw, kept the cut sawdust-free. Trees came down faster, though this was in exchange for an earlier end to lumbering in the area.

In 1893, Mashek moved his operation to Whitefish Bay, where there were more forests to fell, and Lily Bay lost its heart and soul. With lumbering over, Lily Bay men turned full time to fishing, an industry that had shared the pier for a long while. They did well for a number of years with herring and whitefish. In the days before refrigeration, herring was pickled, and a cooper's shop was needed to produce the fifty-five to sixty barrels shipped out each year to Cleveland, Chicago and Kansas City. Later, when refrigeration became available, the production of barrels switched to wood boxes for frozen fish.

For so long, Lily Bay was able to adapt to the changing needs of the business world, but eventually, the town came to an end. All that remains today is the Lily Bay Sawmill and the old Wester's Fish House, now a private residence.

Lily Bay dissolved to less than a ghost town. So, too, the firm of Hanson and Scove ended prematurely when Hans Scove died on March 22, 1889, of tuberculosis. In Scove's absence, other manufacturers finally had a chance to make a name for themselves in Manitowoc. We have one last ship of theirs to discuss, however.

The auxiliary gas schooner *James H. Hall* was built in Manitowoc in 1885 by Hanson and Scove at the behest of wheat dealer and alderman Samuel S. Hall (1832–1914), who named the ship after his eldest son. The length was ninety-one feet, with twenty-two feet of breadth, and it had a capacity for 100 tons. Captain Christian D. Christiansen (1845–1915) of Manitowoc first commanded the vessel for Hall before later becoming the sole owner. After almost thirty years, Christiansen sold the *Hall* to horse dealer Samuel H. Newman (1860–1929) of Algoma in 1913. Newman's success in horses allowed him to expand into lumber, which required more ships.

Although the first years under Newman were apparently successful, the *Hall* had a run of bad luck in 1916. In mid-August, Newman was making a standard crossing from Marinette to Washington Island. Newman was in conversation with his engineer, Gilbert "Gib" Goodletson, and then stepped away for a few minutes while the ship was passing Chambers Island. On return, Goodletson was gone, seemingly fallen overboard, although no one heard a thing. He was presumed drowned, and his body was never recovered. How an experienced seaman fell into Green Bay without notice remains a mystery. Newman was able to finish the short journey himself and dispatched Coast Guard sailors who were on Plum Island, but the search was fruitless. Newman told the press he was so distraught that he planned to quit sailing at the end of the season.

Soon after, the *Hall* was in the bay when the ship hit ground near the Marinette shore. It likely would have gone down, but a pleasure craft saw the distressed vehicle and was able to alert a tug. The *Hall* was removed before considerable damage could be had.

Less than a month after this, the ship ran aground again at the very shallow Twin River Point, sometimes known as the "Graveyard of the Lakes" and today called Rawley Point. As the original name suggests, Twin River Point is an area just offshore from the city of Two Rivers, north of Manitowoc. Whether the incident happened at night is not made clear, but the 113-foot Rawley Point Lighthouse was well kept by Everett Charles Sterritt (1873–1934), who was always at the ready to sound his steam-powered foghorn. A second, smaller lighthouse was also in the vicinity. Vessels were generally considered lost when damaged there, but through some miracle the captain was able to navigate to a shipyard in Door County. The smaller lighthouse, the Two Rivers North Pierhead Light, is today on display at the city's Fishing Village Museum.

While the *Hall* was being attended to, Newman was followed by what the newspaper called "a great big unreasonable jinx." During a leisurely drive around town, his Hudson automobile collided with a Hagemeister brewery truck. Newman's vehicle was damaged to the point that an axle broke and a wheel rolled away. Perhaps Newman was better off avoiding cars and boats and sticking with horses.

The *James Hall* was repaired and "released from the boxes" at Sturgeon Bay on September 30, 1916. The next day, Seavey came to town and made an offer to Sam Newman on the ship. He appeared on behalf of himself and his business partner, attorney Newton C. Spencer of Escanaba. By October 2, the sale was completed and Seavey set off for Bark River. The press noted that if only Dame Fortune would smile on Seavey, he could be rich; the man was "a hustler from the word go." Dame Fortune was not smiling, and the *James Hall*'s misadventures returned a mere month later.

Carrying eighty-five thousand feet of lumber from Thompson, Michigan, for James Root Andrews of Escanaba, the *James H. Hall* met its demise at the mouth of Thunder River at Alpena, Michigan, on Lake Huron on November 6, 1916. Captain Seavey tried to escape a terrible, windy storm, with gusts at fifty-six miles an hour, but his attempt to seek shelter backfired and was his undoing. Aiming for a channel of the Thunder River, he miscalculated in the wind and was off by fifty feet. The *Hall* burned to a total loss and was abandoned. One source says it struck a stone pier prior to burning, splitting in two and literally getting "pounded to pieces." It was equipped with an auxiliary gas engine, which was suspected of contributing to its fiery loss.

Another report came that the ship was taking on water through a defective hatch and Seavey attempted to save the *Hall* by detouring to Saginaw Bay, but he was too late. Saginaw Bay is the large bay giving the Michigan mitten its thumb and is a good deal south of Alpena. Either way, the end result was the same. Somehow, the lumber was saved and continued to its destination at Bay City, but the boat (valued at $7,000) was a total loss.

The *Door County Democrat* recounted the end of the *Hall* on November 24, adding one more piece of the story: it claimed that reports announced "two lives lost" in the sinking though declined to offer the names. As near as can be told, this was a false report. The crew—Seavey, Frank Beard, Joseph and Pete Nedeau—was instead rescued by the tugboat *Ralph*, with Captain Richard William Piepkorn at the helm. Piepkorn directed them to a hotel, where they enjoyed dry clothes and a warm supper.

Following the end of the *James Hall*, Seavey pivoted to a forty-foot motor launch named the *Mary Alice* around 1917. The *Mary Alice* was built in 1912 and had formerly been owned by a man named Pickard in Green Bay. You might recall that Seavey had previously sailed in the *Wanderer*; what became of this ship is something of a mystery. Some accounts—though not contemporary—say the ship was destroyed by fire in 1918, shortly before Seavey purchased the *Mary Alice*. They may be conflating the *Wanderer* with the *James Hall*. Other sources say he sold it to someone on Washington Island as far back as 1911. With his new craft, did Seavey continue as a marshal or an outlaw, or both, or neither? The record is slim, but motor launches were a favorite of Great Lakes smugglers when Prohibition began, putting him in the right position for some easy money.

Overall, 1917 was a quiet year for Seavey, but not without suspicions of murder coming his way once again. On April 24, a Northwestern dock employee named John Hoffman disappeared, and a multiweek search began, with some pointing blame at Captain Dan. The Luxemburger Society (of which Hoffman was a member) made a search of Delta County. Sheriff Iverson and his deputies made inquiries. A rumor was heard that a man matching Hoffman's description was seen on Seavey's boat. Iverson questioned Seavey and searched the former Ford River mill, where Seavey was spending his time. Iverson was convinced that the man on Seavey's boat was not Hoffman. On day nine of Hoffman's disappearance, the belief shifted from foul play to accident: perhaps he merely had a heart attack and fell off the dock while fishing? His body would wash up sooner or later.

Sailor John Mitchell first met Seavey soon after he acquired the *Mary Alice*. Mitchell recalled that the "rough and ready lawless days were gone" but Seavey was still involved in "the girl business." Seavey was "still a big burly man, a bit paunchy, sparse red hair and huge freckled hands." His handshake was still strong, and his voice was booming, and one was wise to avoid Seavey when "his gait was unsteady." Mitchell says: "I remember going over to Stonington dock in my sloop Venus when Dan was there with a high school picnic. He warned me to get started back as we were in for a heavy west wind, pointing out the high flying clouds traveling fast out of the west. At that time he told me how he loved to see the Venus sailing on the bay, that the sight of a vessel under sail gave him the same thrills when one looked up at a flag whipping in the breeze. So he was not without his sentimental side."

Dan's daughter Blanche Seavey married Joseph Callaway of Austria on February 4, 1919, in Delta County. Did Dan attend? This seems likely, being in his own neck of the words. But overall, Seavey was laying low; he managed to stay out of the newspapers throughout all of 1918, only to return in August 1919.

"Captain Dan, like the ghosts of old Captain Kidd…like the old pirate of fiction, he won't stay dead," opined the *Door County Advocate*. It recounted the rumor he had died years ago in a cottage fire on Beaver Island. "No trace of the old sea dog was found for some time," it reported, "and his friends had believed him to go to Davy Jones' locker." This was perhaps a gross repetition of the sawmill misadventure. The newspaper noted how he could have died yet again when the *James Hall* went down, but he merely stayed out of sight somehow, doing who knows what. Now he returned with the *Mary Alice*, "a quiet little gasoline cruiser," and was in the fruit trade.

Roaring Dan's father, Porter Seavey, died in Norway, Maine, on September 28, 1919, at seventy-three years of age. The cause of death was given as "apoplexy" (stroke) and senility. In his final days he fell into a coma and was treated by Mrs. Stephen G. McAllister. Did Dan travel to Maine for the funeral? That is doubtful. Perhaps he never even knew of his father's passing. More likely daughter Jennie attended; according to Seavey's obituary, he had lived with her for a while in Delray, Florida, but preferred the Maine climate.

This boathouse, now in Escanaba, is the only building left from the Squaw Point Lighthouse. *Author's photo.*

The *Mary Alice*, which the newspapers called "one of the classiest and best equipped gas boats on the bay," was back on the water in April 1920. The plan was to transport cargo around the Bay de Nocquet, but Dan would also be taking out people for "moonlight sailing" and picnics. By July, he was regularly taking "berry pickers" out on pleasure trips. He constructed a dock at Squaw Point, across the bay from Gladstone, to attract potential customers to the boat.

Today, Squaw Point can still be found on a map, but if one were to travel there, one would find very little at all. Within a few decades before Seavey arrived there, the prospects were much different. A note from the local county board in 1891 declared:

> *It is stated that the plans of the Minneapolis, Sault Ste. Marie and Atlantic Railroad, now in process of execution, will give to Gladstone the most important shipping in these waters, and that every year will augment its importance. It is stated that last year nearly 300 vessels entered that harbor, and it is expected that next year the number will exceed 1,000. A light*

*either on Sanders Point or Squaw Point will answer the purpose of guiding
into Gladstone Harbor, at least for the present. It is estimated that a site can
be obtained and proper structures can be erected for the establishment of a
proper light at a cost of $10,000.*

On March 2, 1895, the sum of $5,000 was appropriated to establish a
light at or near Squaw Point, and the following year, an acre of land was
purchased for $750. The light was established on August 16, 1897. A drive
well was put down, a nonfreezing pump was provided and a box and platform
built around it. A flagpole was set up, supplies were furnished and another
lighthouse was born. The lighthouse itself, along with the attached keeper's
house, were built with Milwaukee's famous Cream City brick.

Lemuel Marvin served as the keeper beginning in 1897 but tragically
passed away from pneumonia a mere six months later. His widow, Kate
Marvin, took control for the next six years (1898–1904) and was quite the
brave woman, surpassing even Escanaba's Mary Terry. Of the couple's ten
children, four were still young enough to require attention, and in the case
of emergency, there was no house for six miles, or the slightly faster twenty-
minute row to Gladstone if the weather was calm. Ferdinand Ollhoff was
the keeper for the final ten years (1904–14) before acetylene was introduced
and the light became automated.

The lighthouse was still in operation at the time Seavey constructed his
dock. On the evening of August 8, 1921, the entire wood roof, floors and
other flammable parts of the brick dwelling at Squaw Point Light Station
were destroyed by fire. The brick tower was practically uninjured except
the wood finish surrounding window openings. The cast-iron stairs were
exposed to intense heat but were not injured. The glass of the lantern
house was entirely destroyed by heat. The estimated cost of repairs was
$600. How crucial the light was at this point is hard to say. Gladstone
did not see the exponential growth expected at the time of construction,
and the lighthouse appeared in subsequent reports only when the building
became the frequent target of vandals. The building was ultimately torn
down in the 1960s and replaced by a light on a pole before that, too,
was removed.

As the 1920 boating season began, it was predicted to be the slowest year on
record. Only one ship was expected to make the regular Big Bay–Escanaba
run, and that was the Jacobson gas boat known as the *Burger*. Seavey's *Mary
Alice* was expected to take pleasure cruises but not have a regular route. The
only other two boats that were out with any frequency were the *Belle C*,

a Stonington mail craft, and the *Elide*, which spent its time patrolling the fishing waters of the Hansen and Jensen firm.

The *Mary Ethel* of Marinette announced it would make scheduled trips to Garden, Fayette and other ports along the bay, but after only two days in May, the crew packed up and left. The *Burger* was free to take as many jobs as the crew pleased. Commercial fisherman Peter Jensen, a Republican legislator from Delta County, was at the same time trying to get the Soo Line to build a station at Isabella, twelve miles from Garden, to help the farmers of the area have more options for shipping out their produce. But the railroads, much like the boats, could see that the economy was shrinking.

Jensen likely knew he was fighting a losing battle. "The automobile and truck have taken away the business which used to belong to the small steamboat," Jensen said. "I do not believe a boat line serving the small ports near Escanaba ever can be made to pay, financially."

Local historian Raymond E. McDonald collected stories and memories from many old-timers in his book *Four Islands: A History of Detroit, Rock, St. Martins, and Washington Islands*. A representative character is that of Nels Jepson.

A Dane by birth, Jepson came to Wisconsin as a young man in the 1860s and took up work in a Marinette sawmill. As we have already seen, lumber was big business, particularly with the Midwest's population boom of European immigrants. The demand grew even more following the Chicago fire of 1871. Countless ships sailed from Marinette to Chicago with raw material for rebuilding. Chicago being primarily marsh and prairie land, the region had few forests of its own.

Once he had saved up enough money, Jepson purchased his own ship and became a fisherman among the islands beyond the tip of the Door County peninsula. This decision was crystallized one night when Jepson left out a net near Detroit Island and pulled up one thousand pounds of fish in the morning. Over the years, Jepson owned a long list of fishing ships: the *Union*, the *Mary RN*, the *Lettie May*, the *Dolphin*, the *Christiana*, the *Cynthia Gordon* and, finally, the *Bessie Louise*. Jepson could always sell his catches to the Albert Kalmbach Fish Company in Sturgeon Bay.

The years went by, and around 1919, Jepson decided to retire. His wife had passed, his children had grown and he would be far less lonely in Escanaba than floating around, back and forth between the islands of Green Bay. The *Bessie Louise* spent its final days anchored outside Escanaba.

At this point, Dan Seavey enters the tale. McDonald tells of how Seavey tried to upgrade his boat through intimidation.

It was probably the summer of 1920. Nels Jepson was tied up in a slip close to Escanaba and just ahead of him was another gas boat, which was owned by Dan Seavey. They had known each other from years before. Dan liked Nels's boat and wanted to make a deal with him—an even trade, which Nels was not in favor of since his boat was a much better one than Dan's. However, it was not easy to refuse Dan. He had a very persuasive way of getting what he wanted. Nels knew this and he wanted no confrontation with Dan. The trade and Dan worried him. He was not a young man anymore, so it was not easy to cope with this problem. He wanted to leave Escanaba, but he needed gas. Nels wanted to make a move because Dan was getting persistent, and he did not have much time. If he put in gasoline during the day, Dan would see him.

And, if Dan saw him, he would figure Nels was planning to leave for the vicinity of Washington Island without trading vessels.

Nels waited until Dan was busy in the saloon one dark night and sneaked out of the harbor under sail. He coasted out of the harbor in a light wind, which took a while and made Jepson nervous, and when he reached the buoy at the harbor entrance, he cranked up the engine and headed out to Green Bay, hoping his gas would last to Washington Island. He made it all the way in to his dock in Detroit Harbor. McDonald says, "Nels was a happy man to have gotten away from Dan so easily and to still have his boat." Jepson eventually moved once again to Marinette, never returning to Escanaba or running into Seavey again. He was buried on Washington Island.

Daniel and his wife, Anna, lived at a rented home at 512 Hale Street (today, Second Avenue South) in Escanaba in 1920. He told the census taker that his occupation was being the captain of his own boat.

When asked by the newspapers in April 1921, Seavey said he was considering going on the Big Bay-Escanaba route for the summer. He was planning on special excursions, but no one that year had yet announced boat service to Fayette, Garden or Fairport from Escanaba.

Seavey and the *Mary Alice* switched gears to cherries in July 1922, making runs between Escanaba and Sturgeon Bay. Seavey told the press he was saddened to halt his "pleasure party service," but a large number of earnest customers requested cherries, and he had to go where the money was. He would make runs to Sturgeon Bay, charging passengers who wanted a ride to pick their own, and then purchasing whatever he could haul to sell back in Escanaba. The second week of cherry season saw

Seavey in the Sturgeon Bay Boat Works getting the *Mary Alice* fixed up for damage received below the water line.

Door County cherries have become an icon of the county, and for good reason. Following the clearing of timber, farmers found the soil was not adequate for the usual crops of wheat or other grains. Things began to turn around in the 1860s, when Joseph Zettle (1846–1925) started planting apple trees in the shallow soils and found that the trees flourished. Soon, the fruit growers of Wisconsin took notice. The University of Wisconsin's Horticulture Department began testing various fruits to determine an ideal crop for the county. Apples, plums and pears were all planted, but the ultimate success was found in 1896, when their tart cherry crop greatly exceeded expectations. Within fifty years, Door County would harvest 10 percent of the annual cherries grown in the United States.

With an increase in production, reaching a point that more fresh cherries were produced than the local communities could eat, the county began shipping the cherries to markets nationwide. An old pea-canning plant was converted into what became, at the time, the world's largest cherry-canning plant. Even during the Great Depression, the cherry orchards were able to continue profiting by promoting the cherries through great marketing.

The *Mary Alice* took six men out fishing east of Drummond Island, in the Canadian border waters, on July 25, 1922, and it serves as a great example for how the pleasure trips operated. The party came back to Escanaba with the limit on muskie and black bass. One of the muskies weighed forty-eight pounds. The men were: real estate broker John Aloysius Semer, Mike Aley, W.H. Kennedy, lumber company superintendent Omar Clyde Curtis, Tom Thompson and M. Collins.

Using a grappling hook, a cable and a windlass, Seavey was able to retrieve 45 fathoms (270 feet) of anchor chain and anchor, weighing more than six tons, to the surface near the no. 1 ore dock in Escanaba on August 14. The chain, estimated to be worth $3,500, was returned to the steamer *J.A. Campbell*. Not long before, the chain had come loose from the steamer *Mills*. While it took three days of dragging to find where the chain had settled, the retrieval was done in under three hours. The newspaper expected that Seavey would receive a third of the value (over $1,000) as a reward. Seavey told the press that 1922 had been a good summer; beyond the odd jobs and cherry runs, the black bass had been plentiful, too.

The *Mary Alice* changed its cargo once more that season, when, on September 1, the ship arrived in Escanaba packed full of Michigan free-stone peaches of the Crawford variety. Seavey was able to ask $0.50 per basket. For the remainder of the season, Seavey pledged to make runs between Frankfort and Escanaba with peaches, plums and pears. The yield had been particularly good, and peaches could be purchased for as low as $1.50 a bushel. How many baskets were in a bushel is not known, but so long as the number was four or more, the profit margin was quite healthy.

In March 1923, Seavey and his business partner, attorney James C. Baker (with his wife, Mabel O. Baker), purchased a 386-acre tract of land at Gouley's Harbor on the Garden Peninsula from John S. Mills to establish a sportsmen's club. Gouley's Harbor is an isolated inlet on the Garden Peninsula, in the vicinity of the Garden Bluff. If the name *Mills* sounds familiar, it is because he was involved in the sawmill explosion episode eight years prior.

Mary P. Gouley (born 1848) was an enterprising pioneer who lived on the Garden Peninsula in the late nineteenth century. She was said to be a friendly, well-educated woman who was also an accomplished musician. Following his death, Mary inherited a large tract of land from Leon Trombly (1830–1873), an uncle with whom she had lived for some years. Trombly, from Bay City, Michigan, acquired the property through a land grant only a few years before in 1868. (The Trombly/Tromble family was the first to settle in Bay County; incidentally.) This Upper Peninsula land included the Garden Bluff, a massive limestone outcrop. The rugged shoreline beneath these capes contains several small, remote coves and river estuaries. One isolated inlet became known as Gouley's Harbor after Mary Gouley built her home and farmed the fertile lands on top of the bluff, once cultivated by local Indians. She was also a shrewd business owner who ventured into logging, milling and quarrying. The last one in particular is how she made her name.

In 1880, Gouley reportedly discovered high-quality dolomite on her property, as well as some sandstone and marble deposits. She sent samples of these stones to Chicago for testing and polishing, and they were subsequently rated as excellent building material. Geologically, dolomite (now often called dolostone) is a close cousin of limestone, usually containing larger amounts of calcium and magnesium. This brings a denser, harder, variable crystalline structure to the rock that often takes a fine polish.

Marble is formed by the chemical change of calcite or dolomite through recrystallization of the component minerals and comes in a variety of colors, including brown, green, white, black and various shades of blue. Mary Gouley reportedly had a marketable bluish-gray dolomitic marble on her property. It should be noted that the "market definition" of marble departs

The stone cliffs in the Garden Peninsula provided marble and limestone for construction. *Author's photo.*

somewhat from the classic geological description, in that marketers usually accept as marble almost any limestone that can be polished to a sufficient degree. Gouley opened her stone quarry at least as early as 1882, offering product through ads in local newspapers and by brokers in the Chicago area. The advertisements were saturating the newspapers around 1890.

Some of Gouley's business transactions were briefly described in the early *Iron Port* newspaper of Escanaba, and county commissioner Thomas C. Elegeert (1941–2017), a board member of the local historical society, has excerpted and published selected clippings. These excerpts clearly document that Gouley provided stone for the foundation of the courthouse in Escanaba and for the John Villiers Farwell (1825–1908) mansion in Chicago, as well as for various other Midwest building projects. However, the exact amounts of stone removed from the quarry (or its precise location) are not disclosed in those articles. Available information suggests that Gouley worked the quarry for about ten years but then closed up shop before the end of the nineteenth century. The fact that Gouley supplied building stone for the Chicago mansion of John Farwell is in itself a significant event.

The Farwell brothers, John and Charles, were extremely important figures in Midwest American history. Charles Benjamin Farwell (1823–1903) was Chicago's first "political boss" and is recognized as the creator of the "Chicago political machine." He eventually became a powerful Republican U.S. senator who used his influence to channel much of the nation's business through Chicago enterprises. John Farwell was a dry-goods merchant who organized and operated an immense mercantile distribution system to send products throughout the United States and especially to the expanding western frontier. For some time, he partnered with Marshall Field (1834–1906), who went on to create his own department store empire that lasted for over 150 years before being absorbed into Macy's in 2006. In 1882, when the Farwell brothers built side-by-side mansions in Chicago, John's business was doing some $20 million per year and was one of the three largest wholesalers in the country.

The Farwell mansions were constructed on Pearson Street, between Lake Shore Drive and Michigan Avenue. Charles selected a Queen Anne style, whereas John's home was referred to as a "baronial" style; in the latter, the contractor incorporated a poured concrete skeleton, one of the first of its kind. This suggests that the "Gouley Stone" was not used as foundational material but rather as a decorative façade. The mansions stand today, and visitors can see the stonework for themselves.

As noted in an earlier chapter, in the later decades of the nineteenth century, Delta County was a thriving region of the Upper Peninsula, with booming interests in lumbering, mining and shipping. In the early 1880s, Escanaba, now incorporated as a city and the judicial seat of the county, was in desperate need of a regional courthouse and improvements to the existing jail, infirmary and schoolhouse. A tax levy for these projects was proposed and met with some debate, but the courthouse construction went forth under the supervision of the J.B. Sweath Company for the sum of $21,900. Year-round work started in 1882 and concluded with official occupancy in 1884.

The finished building was a notable structure, Victorian in style with high windows, vaulted ceilings and a unique circular staircase. Although the courthouse suffered a serious fire in 1901, it served the county well until 1961, when the building was torn down. Three different stones were used in the construction of the building, which reportedly had a very deep basement. The walls beneath the water table were built of local stone from Duck Creek and were directly laid without any particular facing. This same stone was used at the level of the water table for walls and windowsills, except that it was smoothed and shaped by hand with a hammer for a more finished appearance. Dolomite from Gouley's quarry, polished and hammer-faced, formed the basement wall and was cemented in place with a slight front-to-back slope; each block was faced to promote a very close fit. The aboveground foundation, as well as the window and door trimming, were done in what was called polished "Bridgeport Stone," apparently an amalgamation of New England granite.

While digging a well at Garden Bluff in June 1923, Seavey uncovered some unusual artifacts: a tempered copper chisel, an Indian "medicine rock," a war hatchet and several high-quality arrowheads. The chisel, found six feet underground, rang like a brass bell and showed all the signs of being tempered—something uncommon if it were a native artifact. At this point, Seavey was well on his way to finishing his club, which he called Bass Harbor. He had constructed multiple docks and a two-story cabin and claimed to be able to serve up to a dozen guests at a time. He offered fresh vegetables and other options he described as "straight from the farm." Seavey told the press that his docks were open to anyone—for free—not just his guests, and he hoped local residents would pay him a visit.

Dan Seavey was forced to make a clarification in February 1924, explaining that while his docks were free, his fish were not. He was ready to "make war" on those he considered to be "poachers." He claimed that the law gave him exclusive fishing rights within one mile of his property and that anyone caught violating this would be prosecuted. Seavey shared the following letter with the press that he had received from his friend and attorney James Baker:

> *I understand you are still having trouble with other fishermen who are setting their nets near the shore of Garden Bluff, where you have your own nets. Notify these people that they must keep their gill nets outside of the one mile limit from the shore of Garden Bluff. Act No. 7640 of the Compiled Laws of 1915 provides as follows: "It shall be unlawful for any person to place or drive any mound net piles or stakes, or any other species or seines or posts, or build any platform or piers, or any species of seines of continuous trap net, gill nets to one mile from the beach or shore, the low water mark at the lake straits, inlets and bays on the sail water fronting such owner or occupant's land." As we own the Riparian rights around Garden Bluff, this ownership gives us the right to prevent fishing within one mile from our shore. As we are fishing ourselves, we have a double right to prevent other fishermen from interfering with our own fishing. We will have these people arrested for trespass if they do not stop, and whenever you advise that this be done, I will start necessary procedure.*

The sportsmen's club never materialized while Seavey was there, and his interest in the land was sold to Alfred Clinton Hoy (1882–1948) of Chicago in July 1924. Attorney James Baker maintained his half of the ownership. Rumors were circulating that the property would no longer be a sportsmen's club but instead be transformed into a summer camp with shares sold to various prominent Chicagoans. Baker told the press: "I am not prepared to make a definite announcement at this time. We have some attractive offers. The development of the [400 acre] tract along lines that will bring the best results for the entire peninsula community is just as important as any of the other phases of the transaction. We want to do the thing that will be best for the community in general, as well as for ourselves." Seavey, for his part, told the press that he was stepping away from the business because of "failing health."

Today, the Bass Harbor property is a land conservancy called the Garden Bluff Trust. During a review of title transactions for acreage, a fascinating quit-claim deed was found. The document stated that "Mary Silver" waived all dower rights to the property being purchased by "John Silver," also known as Dan Seavey. Presumably, the "Mary" in this document refers to Seavey's first wife from decades prior. Richard Boyd suggests that "this deed discloses that they were never legally divorced," which would make his two additional marriages bigamous. In case you missed the reference, Seavey's nickname was a clear nod to "Long John" Silver, the fictional pirate.

In May 1926, the *Mary Alice* spent time at the Sturgeon Bay Boat Works for repairs and painting. That summer was uneventful and marked Seavey's final season on the lake. The following spring, Seavey sold the forty-foot boat to a resident of Gladstone, Michigan. Seavey was said to be retiring because of a gasoline explosion that had paralyzed his right arm.

Anne Bradley Seavey died from pulmonary edema (fluid in the lungs) on April 2, 1928, at 211 South Sixth Street in Escanaba after being ill for three weeks; she was fifty years old. Sadly, her death certificate lists her as "Mrs. Dan Seavey," giving her no identity of her own. Survivors were her mother, Caroline Brown; brother Allen Marvin Bradley; and sisters Lottie May (Daniel) Malloy and Charlotte Elizabeth (Elmer) Ellsworth, all of Manistique. Reverend John B. Hubbard, a Presbyterian minister, conducted a service at the Allo Funeral Home before the burial at Lake View Cemetery in Escanaba.

Blanche Seavey-Callaway was married again on July 2, 1928, in Delta County to Edward Broed, the son of Henry and Fanny Tayzag Broed. The ceremony was conducted by Lutheran pastor Richard J. Peterson, with

Arnold and May Johnson of Iron Mountain serving as witnesses. Again, we may ask if Dan was present. The simple truth is that, unless photographs surface, we will never know.

At the end of his career, Seavey allegedly accepted a position with the United States Marshals Service, where he worked to curb poaching, smuggling and piracy on Lake Michigan. On one occasion, he found a wanted smuggler (said to be "stealing everything in sight") in Naubinway, an unincorporated town in Mackinac County. The man, bringing booze to local Indians, allegedly told Seavey, "If you can drag me outside [of this tavern], I'll board your schooner for Chicago." A fight broke out. Seavey won by pinning his victim under a piano, and the wanted man died the next day. Boyd has this as a Bureau of Indian Affairs position, not a U.S. Marshal position, which may be likely given Seavey's earlier association with the BIA. Would the U.S. Marshals even hire a man they had once carried off in chains?

William Duchaine embellishes the tale a bit more:

> *The battle started. Several hours later, the saloon was a total wreck. Every once in a while the fighters would stop for a drink of whiskey. What with the fighting and the drinks Dan began worrying about the supply and decided to finish the affair. His opponent went down and Dan put a piano on his neck. Then, reconsidering, he removed the piano and invited the vanquished to have a drink, before resuming the fight. It was too late, and the man died the next day. Dan turned him over to be buried, sent in his report and went free.*

Neither Boyd nor Duchaine name the man or identify the date, and outside of these two variations, no concrete source, such as a newspaper article, was found.

Dan, now a widower, lived with daughter Josephine in Sagola, Dickinson County, Michigan, throughout 1930. Josephine, using the surname Beauchamp, did not live with her husband. The census identifies Seavey as the captain of a "marine boat," while Josephine is unemployed. In February 1930, a newspaper reporter visited Seavey at his daughter's home. The reporter asked Seavey what he thought of the news that gold was recently found in both Alaska and Arizona. "I'm not a bit interested in gold rushes," said the sailor. "I invested $10,000 and 18 months of my time in a gold mine in Alaska back in the late nineties and came back broke." He then proceeded to tell stories found elsewhere in this book.

In the early 1930s, Dan lived for a while at Martha Ann Champ Wead's boardinghouse at 319 Ludington in Escanaba, an area today populated by government offices. He would relate tales to newspaper writers, such as the time he led an expedition to Nipigon, near Thunder Bay, to look for ancient ruins with a certain Professor Steadman of the University of Missouri. Seavey also led researchers from the University of Wisconsin to Indian mounds near Lake Noquebay in Marinette County, as well as in Green Valley, Wisconsin, near Shawano.

He further claimed to have been the stunt double for an actress playing a diver in an early Hollywood movie. As Seavey described it, the scene was filmed near Sturgeon Bay and concerned the wrecking of an ore carrier on the Great Lakes. "All I got for about three weeks work in the movies was salt pork and beans, and I was promised that a check would be sent to me from Chicago," Seavey explained. "The check never came." Boyd suggests the movie might be 1920's *Below the Surface*, starring Hobart Bosworth. Further still, Seavey actually claimed to be a cousin of Bosworth. One reporter reached out to Bosworth, who said he had no cousins named Seavey and did not want any. Though a Seavey-Bosworth relation may be untrue, Dan was in fact a distant cousin of Western author Louis L'Amour (1908–1988).

Yet another story claims that Seavey stole skulls from an Indian burial ground and used them to scare barflies away from their drinks, but no reliable source for this claim exists today (beyond his loose connection to Indian mounds mentioned earlier). William Duchaine claims that one woman offered Seavey $100 to scare her husband with the skull until he gave up drinking altogether. John Mitchell goes even further, saying that a rumor persisted that Seavey "drowned an Indian in Ogontz Bay." The man had boarded the *Wanderer* looking for his wife and daughter, who he believed had been kidnapped by Seavey.

Mitchell further tells the tale of "Jesse Gouley of Ford River," who "knew Seavey and sailed with him on a little gasboat named the Rose of Garden. He said Dan was always turning up with a new boat, most of them, Jesse suspected, were stolen from someplace on the lake and later resold. He refused to go with Dan on one such expedition, at which Dan showed him a big roll of currency, cursed Jesse for a lily-livered longshoreman, and from then on would have nothing to do with him."

Duchaine says that Seavey was not all bad.

Dan had a warm place in his heart for boys, and there are several stories told of his kind treatment of them. On one of many occasions when they were taking apples from his schooner by spearing them with darts tied to strings and lifting the apples to the dock, he filled a bushel basket with the fruit and passed it up to them on the wharf, at the same time giving them a lecture about stealing. The boys who loved the sea were his favorites.

Another story tells of a youngster whose father had warned him to keep away from the harbor in general, and Dan Seavey in particular. The parent, having caught his son leaving the dock, was giving him a spanking. The boy yelled loudly, promising never to see Dan Seavey again. Suddenly a heavy hand fell upon the father's shoulder, and before he knew what was happening, Dan was giving him what he had been giving his son. "That will teach you to leave my shipmates alone," growled the Captain.

This last one parallels an anecdote later told by Mitchell. "Seavey himself told me the story of the rich man's son who wanted to ship aboard the Wanderer at Escanaba," he recalled.

*This young lad was entranced with Capt. Seavey, the **Wanderer** and the rough and romantic life. Dan took a liking to him and paid the boy 50 cents a day to help unload the schooner's cargo of fruit. One night when the boy left the ship, Dan saw him pass under the light at Oliver's coal shed, where he was seized by an older man who started scuffling with him. Dan leaped ashore and rushed into the scuffle thinking the man was trying to rob the youngster, and after administering a good beating to the ruffian, the boy trying all the while to stop him, and finally making him understand that the man was his father, who was punishing him for hanging around such a ruffian as Dan. Dan said he picked the man up and apologized, and told the boy from then on to stay away from him.*

Mitchell believed the boy was Fred Royce, who founded the Escanaba Yacht Club (EYC) with him, though he does not say why this was his suspicion. Incidentally, another EYC founder was Coroner Bartley—small world.

From 1935 to 1940, Dan was the head of household at Grover, Marinette County. No addresses were given in the census, but Seavey was said to be "on relief." His daughter Josephine and son-in-law W.A. Wood (born 1888) lived with him. W.A. was a lumberman; Josephine was a cook in a hotel.

The Bosworth rumor, like all Seavey rumors, refused to die. On January 20, 1946, a letter from Mrs. John Haring of Bark River appeared in the Escanaba newspaper. "Of late you haven't mentioned Captain Dan Seavey," she noted. "I wonder if it would interest you to know that Dan and the late Hobart C. Bosworth, well-known movie actor, were first cousins, and indeed bore a striking resemblance to each other. Dan never missed seeing a picture shown here featuring Bosworth." The editor consulted their "Seavey file" and found that this claim had been made before and that the newspaper had even questioned Bosworth. The actor denied knowing who Seavey was and said he had no first, second or third cousins named Seavey. By 1961, this rumor not only persisted but also grew. John Mitchell said Seavey "was reputed to be the half-brother" of Bosworth!

In 1948, the former Mary Seavey married her third husband, Frank Satka, who was from Winona, Minnesota. Satka occasionally used the alias "Frank Hintz." In fact, most of the Satka family changed their name to Hintz for an unknown reason. The couple lived in a small house near the Ace of Spades in Sagola.

Dan Seavey died at the Eklund convalescent (nursing) home at 310 Oconto Avenue in Peshtigo at 10:30 a.m. on February 14, 1949, at the supposed age of eighty-three. He had been ill since the previous November. According to news reports, the old rascal turned religious in his final days and would read from a Bible previously owned by Mary Gouley. The nursing home was renamed the Pel-Bar Convalescent Home in 1960.

The funeral was conducted at the Zeitler funeral home, with Reverend John Francis, a methodist minister, leading the service. Seavey is buried in Forest Home Cemetery, Marinette. His pallbearers were farmer George Lund, milkman Earl P. Seymour, tavernkeeper Lester McDonald, farmer Robert Jandt, farmer Carl Hart and farmer William Denis Bashford. Aside from being primarily farmers, these men had another thing in common: they all lived in the small community of Grover, suggesting they were men Seavey met in the final stage of his life.

Those attending the funeral included Mrs. Fred Habaner, Mrs. Joseph Theisen of Waucedah, Nancy and Lila Gould of Loretto, Mollie Newhouse, Mrs. Frieda Newhouse Parker, Ione Cook and locomotive engineer Fred Joseph Adriansen of Green Bay. Cook was the adopted sister of Mollie and Frieda Newhouse. The connection these folks had to Seavey is unknown, though Anne Seavey's sister married a Gould. There is no word if they were related to the Albert Gould who Seavey had once thrown in the lake.

Mary Plumley Seavey Satka followed her three husbands to the beyond in 1965 at age ninety-three in Sagola. She is buried alongside Frank Satka in nearby Channing.

Dan Seavey's final resting place. *Findagrave.*

Seavey's closest daughter, Josephine Wood, died at St. Francis Hospital in Escanaba on October 26, 1979, from arteriosclerosis. In her final days, she could no longer swallow without medical assistance. She had no children of her own. Josephine was survived by four half sisters: Mrs. Delphine Steele Childers of Ranier, Mrs. Malvina Steele Burns of Sagola, Mrs. Rose Steele Brunelle of Escanaba and Mrs. Manda Steele (William) Dishaw of Wauceedah, Wisconsin. Josephine was buried in Forest Home Cemetery, Marinette, next to her father.

Despite his legendary status, no statue or plaque exists marking the life of "Roaring Dan" Seavey—not even a historical marker on one of Lake Michigan's many docks and beaches. His grave, unlike that of his son, is modest and nondescript. Even those intentionally looking for it will more than likely spend a great deal of time wandering the cemetery grounds fruitlessly. Yet, his name lives on without monuments. When researching this book, I would run into people who instantly recognized the Seavey name and were quick to point me in the right direction or offer a larger-than-life rumor. As a historian, I hope Seavey's life is preserved accurately for generations; as someone who enjoys a good fish tale, I hope the stories only continue to grow with time. Long live the pirate of Lake Michigan!

A NOTE ON SOURCES

I first stumbled onto Dan Seavey's story in passing while reading about smuggling and Prohibition-era crime. Being intrigued by the idea of a "pirate" in my own backyard, I looked for more thorough sources. Surprisingly, there were few that went beyond the most general—and inaccurate—telling.

The most comprehensive version to date, as far as I'm aware, is Dr. Richard Boyd's "A Pirate Roams Lake Michigan: The Dan Seavey Story." At only nineteen pages, there was still much to be added, and a number of the sources in there pertain to Seavey's legendary exploits. I had no desire to print anything I could not confirm. In short, Boyd's monograph was a guiding light and should be considered the father of "Seaveyology," but there was much work to be done.

Seavey was covered extensively in the newspapers of Escanaba and Sturgeon Bay, and those articles are really the core of this book. Further articles were found in Manitowoc and to a lesser degree elsewhere, each adding a piece of the puzzle.

The genealogical record of Seavey and his family was accessed directly when possible from courthouse records. The Area Research Center (ARC) at the University of Wisconsin in Green Bay was helpful, holding such original documents as Seavey's will and a Kewaunee County divorce petition. Delta County (Escanaba) housed marriage and death records and what little remains of the 1915 coroner inquest. The county clerk went above and beyond, digging in a dirty basement to retrieve files that could just as well have been thrown out decades ago. For those documents I could not access in person (thanks, COVID-19), I relied on scans provided by the FamilySearch website rather than the originals.

The earliest Seaveys in America are recorded in Charles A. Hazlett's 1915 history of Rockingham County and in genealogies compiled by Elisha Porter Seavey (1838–1913). The Seavey family also appears in the diaries of Reverend Jacob Holt Lovejoy, published by the Bethel Historical Society. For background on the Upper Peninsula, I used a variety of sources, including the books *Escanaba: Iron Port of the World* by Walter R. Nursey and *A History of the Garden Peninsula* by Thomas Edward Jacques.

The memories of Escanaba sailor John Mitchell are kept at the Delta County Historical Society, and they are priceless. As sailors are known to do, he may have embellished here and there, but the firsthand accounts of Seavey are rare, and Mitchell was thoughtful in writing them down for us to enjoy sixty years later!

Many books have been written on the Yukon Gold Rush, but I relied primarily on two: James and Susan Preyde's *Yukon Gold: High Hopes and Dashed Dreams* (Hancock House) and Melody Webb's *Yukon: The Last Frontier* (University of Nebraska Press).

There are literally hundreds or even thousands of books on Lake Michigan and the Great Lakes. Some of the books consulted include the following:

Bogue, Margaret Beattie. *Around the Shores of Lake Michigan: A Guide to Historic Sites*. Madison: University of Wisconsin Press, 1985.

Curwood, James Oliver. *The Great Lakes: The Vessels That Plough Them*. New York: Putnam, 1909.

Harvey, Miles. *The King of Confidence*. New York: Hachette Book Group, 2020.

Jensen, Trygvie. *Through Waves and Gales Come Fisherman's Tales*. N.p.: Cold Harbor Publishing Company, 2009.

Marchetti, Donna. *Lake Michigan: A Guide to Small Towns, Rural Areas and Natural Attractions*. Saginaw, MI: Glovebox Guidebooks, 2000.

McDonald, Raymond E. *Four Islands: A History of Detroit, Rock, St. Martins, and Washington Islands*. Sturtevant, WI: Wolfsong Publications, 1984.

Schumacher, Michael. *November's Fury: The Deadly Great Lakes Hurricane of 1913*. Minneapolis: University of Minnesota Press, 2013.

Shelak, Benjamin J. *Shipwrecks of Lake Michigan*. Black Earth, WI: Trails Books, 2003.

Stonehouse, Frederick. *Haunted Lake Michigan*. Duluth, MN: Lake Superior Port Cities, 2006.

Wardius, Ken, and Barb Wardius. *Wisconsin Lighthouses: A Photographic and Historical Guide.* Madison: Wisconsin Historical Society Press, 2013.

Wright, Larry, and Patricia Wright. *Great Lakes Lighthouses Encyclopedia.* Erin, ON: Boston Mills Press, 2006.

ABOUT THE AUTHOR

By day, Gavin Schmitt works as a historian for Wisconsin's finest library. After sunset, his research turns to crime, the Mafia, unsolved murders and piracy in his home state. Best known as the author of *Milwaukee Mafia*, this is Gavin's ninth nonfiction book of Dairy State history.

Visit us at
www.historypress.com